Lyman Abbott

**The Star of Bethlehem**

Old Testament shadows of New Testament truths

Lyman Abbott

**The Star of Bethlehem**
*Old Testament shadows of New Testament truths*

ISBN/EAN: 9783337038427

Printed in Europe, USA, Canada, Australia, Japan

Cover: Foto ©Lupo / pixelio.de

More available books at **www.hansebooks.com**

# THE STAR OF BETHLEHEM.

## OLD TESTAMENT SHADOWS

OF

## NEW TESTAMENT TRUTHS.

BY LYMAN ABBOTT.

WITH DESIGNS BY DORÉ, DELAROCHE, DURHAM, AND PARSONS.

NEW YORK.
JOHN KNOX McAFEE, PUBLISHER.

158 WEST 23d STREET.

1895.

# PREFACE.

The Old Testament is more full of parables than the New. Its history is prophetic. Its stories are parables in real life. The chronicles of Israel are full of God's foreshadowings of the redemption of the world. From the Fall in Eden to the restoration of the Jews under Ezra, there are, all along the way, finger-posts that point to the Cross of Christ. Their inscriptions are sometimes so plain that the wayfaring man, though a fool, need not err therein. They are sometimes so obscured that the heedless traveler notes them not. These finger-posts I seek to decipher; these parables to interpret.

The light that shines from the Old Testament is that of the Star of Bethlehem, which conducts the reader to the manger of his Incarnate Lord. That star I seek to follow.

# CONTENTS.

### I.
THE CITIES OF THE·PLAIN..................Page 9

"The wages of sin is death; but the gift of God is eternal life through Jesus Christ our Lord."

### II.
WATER IN THE WILDERNESS............................ 23

"If thou knewest the gift of God, and who it is that saith to thee, 'Give me to drink,' thou wouldest have asked of him, and he would have given thee living water."

### III.
ELIEZER'S PRAYER................................ 37

"Whatsoever ye shall ask in my name, that will I do, that the Father may be glorified in the Son."

### IV.
JOSEPH'S STAFF.................................... 49

"We both labor and suffer reproach because we trust in the living God, who is the Savior of all men, especially of those that believe."

### V.
THE GREAT QUESTION................................ 65

"No man can serve two masters; for either he will hate the one and love the other, or else he will hold to the one and despise the other. Ye can not serve God and mammon."

### VI.
THE GREAT DELIVERANCE............................ 81

"Behold the Lamb of God which taketh away the sin of the world."

## VII.
### THE RIVEN ROCK...................................... 99
"But one of the soldiers with a spear pierced his side, and forthwith came there out blood and water."

## VIII.
### THE FIERY SERPENTS AND THE BRAZEN SERPENT: ............ 111
"For he hath made him to be sin for us, who knew no sin; that we might be made the righteousness of God in him."

## IX.
### THE BENEVOLENCE OF BOAZ......................Page 121
"Every good gift and every perfect gift is from above, and cometh down from the Father of lights, with whom is no variableness, neither shadow of turning."

## X.
### THE FORLORN HOPE OF ISRAEL......................... 131
"For ye see your calling, brethren, how that not many wise men, after the flesh, not many mighty, not many noble are called."

## XI.
### THE PRICE OF AMBITION............................ 149
"A man's life consisteth not in the abundance of the things which he possesseth."

## XII.
### SAMSON'S STRENGTH AND WEAKNESS...................... 165
"Denying ungodliness and worldly lusts, we should live soberly, righteously, and godly in this present world; looking for that blessed hope, and the glorious appearing of the great God, and our Savior Jesus Christ."

## XIII.
### ELISHA'S VISION..................................... 177
"We look not at the things which are seen, but at the things which are not seen; for the things which are seen are temporal; but the things which are not seen are eternal."

## XIV.
### THE QUEEN'S CROWN.................................. 193
"Be strong in the Lord, and in the power of his might."

# OLD TESTAMENT SHADOWS.

## I.

### THE CITIES OF THE PLAIN.

THE story of the destruction of Sodom and Gomorrah is one of the most extraordinary in the Old Testament. It is singularly attested by the imperishable witness of the mountains and the sea. Skepticism may scout at the plagues of Egypt; may smile incredulously at the marvelous deliverance of Israel through the Red Sea; may look with ill-concealed pity upon those who, fed daily by God's bounty, believe that God fed the hungry Israelites in the wilderness; may account the stories of the marvels which he wrought in answer to the prayers of Elijah the legends of a romantic age, and reject with ridicule the assertion of the apostle that the effectual fervent prayer of the righteous man availeth much; it will find nowhere in the Bible a story more extraordinary and intrinsically incredible than that of the destruction of the cities of the plain. Yet to deny this, it must not only impugn the sacred writers, but must also repudiate the traditions of heathen nations reported by secular historians, and refuse to listen to the silent testimony of nature itself. For, until the vision of

Ezekiel is fulfilled, and the sacred waters, flowing from God's holy hill, heal the waters of the Salt Sea and give life again to this valley of death—until mercy shall conquer justice in nature as it already has in human experience, this scene of desolation will remain, a terrible witness to the reality of God's justice, and the fearfulness of his judgments.

Nor does it merely testify to the truth of the Scripture narrative. The briny waters of the Salt Sea, the upheaved rocks scored with fire, the mountain of solid salt, the masses of bitumen, the extinct crater of a neighboring volcano, the other innumerable traces of volcanic action, all remain, not only to attest that a remarkable convulsion of nature has taken place in the past, but also to indicate the nature of the phenomenon, and the character of the forces which operated to produce it.

In the southeast corner of Palestine, in a basin scooped out of the solid rock by some extraordinary pre-historic convulsion, lie the waters of what is fitly called the Dead Sea. The barren rocks which environ it crowd close to the water's edge. The almost impassable pathway which leads down their precipitous sides has no parallel even among the dangerous passes of the Alps and the Apennines. From the surface of this singular lake there perpetually arises a misty exhalation, as though it were steam from a vast caldron, kept at boiling point by infernal fires below. No fish play in these deadly waters. When now and then one ventures hither from the Jordan, he pays for his temerity with his life. No birds make here their nests.

No fruits flourish along these inhospitable shores, save the apples of Sodom, fair to the eye, but turning to dust and ashes in the hand of him that plucks them. The few miserable men that still make their home in this accursed valley are dwarfed, and stunted, and sickly, as those that live in the shadowy border land that separates life from death.

Yet this sterile scene possesses a ghastly, corpse-like beauty, even in death, which indicates what its living beauty must have been. Here and there, along its shores, are a few oases, whose fertile soil, abundant vegetation, and luxuriant growth, point us back to the morning when Abraham and Lot stood on the neighboring hill-top, and "beheld all the plain of Jordan, that it was well watered every where, even as the garden of the Lord." For once the southern extremity of the Dead Sea was doubtless a fertile plain. Magnificent mountains encircled it in their arms. The streams that irrigated its surface outnumbered all that were to be found in all the rest of Palestine. A tropical sun drew from a fertile soil a most luxuriant vegetation. The waters of the neighboring lake, then fresh and sweet, were dotted with many a sail, and alive with innumerable fish. A mountain of salt at the southern extremity of the plain supplied the Holy Land with an article even more essential to the Hebrews than to us. Vast veins of bitumen, interwoven in the texture of the soil, supplied them with fuel, with brick, and with a substitute for pitch and tar, and brought to the vale of Siddim a profitable commerce. Kings fought for the possession of this second Eden. Flourishing cities, embowered in all the bloom and verdure of tropical gardens, sprang up in this "Valley of Fields." The fabled glories of Damascus were surpassed by the realities of this terrestrial paradise. The busy hum of industry resounded where now reigns the unbroken stillness of the grave. The fragrance of many gardens loaded the air now heavy with the exhalations of this salty sea. Where now is utter loneliness and hopeless desolation was once a lake country, teeming with life, and exquisite in all the horticultural beauty of an Asiatic garden —the fairest nook in all the fair land of Canaan.

Yet even then death lurked unseen in the midst of this prolific life. Volcanic fires slumbered beneath the carpeted fields. The veins of bitumen only awaited the torch of the Lord to enkindle farm and city in one universal conflagration. The mound of salt was made ready to mingle its properties with the water of the neighboring lake, and turn it from a fount of life to a sea of death. The lake itself only waited the beck of God to overleap its boundaries, and obliterate, with one fierce and irresistible wave, every trace of the civilization of the proud and prosperous cities of the plain. The very luxuriance of their land bred in its inhabitants those vices which belong to a luxurious and enervated people. The record of their shameless iniquity, hinted at in a few brief words in the sacred story, is too infamous to be dilated on. Lewdness ran such riot that strangers were not safe from the perpetration of crimes which modern literature dares not even so much as name. In all the plain not half a score of men could be found whose purity might justify the mercy of God in restraining the fulfillment of his purposes of justice. In the city of Sodom there was but one who, in the general degeneracy of the age, feared God or regarded his law. Often, perhaps, had Lot remonstrated with his fellows—but in vain; often had he sighed for the peace and purity of his pastoral life, yet lacked the courage to return to it in his old age. His fellow-citizens repaid his remonstrances with mob violence. His own son-in-law ridiculed his warnings of divine judgment.

At length the doomed cities filled to the full the measure of their iniquity. The patience of God would wait no longer. Lot, warned of the impending destruction, went forth by night, at the hazard of his life, to save, if possible, at least his own kinsfolk from a fearful death. But he seemed to them as one that mocked. They laughed him to scorn.

It is easy to imagine the replies of the incredulous people. Their descendants employ the same replies to-day. "Sodom and Gomorrah to be destroyed by fire!" cried one; "it is contrary to all our experience. No evidence can convince me of it." "It would be a violation of the laws of nature," said another. "God is too merciful," said a third. "It will be time enough to flee when the fire comes," said a fourth. "I will think of it," said a fifth; "but the subject is one of momentous importance. I can do nothing in haste."

There was no time for delay. The message was delivered. The blood of this people was henceforth upon their own heads. Lot, leaving behind him his country, home, possessions, friends, kinsfolk—poorer far than when he entered the valley where his wealth had been accumulated—his wife and two daughters his sole companions, went forth to commence his life anew, a stranger in a strange land. The rising sun was just beginning to touch the mountain tops with light as they issued from the western gate of the still sleeping city, and commenced to traverse the plain toward the little city of Zoar, the ruins of which are still to be seen among the mountains that skirt the southern edge of the Dead Sea.

The morning sun rose clear and bright. The city woke from its slumbers, and went to its accustomed tasks. Yet on that highest southern peak there hung a heavy cloud. It was there at early sunrise. The air was hot and murky. A strange oppressiveness was in it. The crowing cock hailed the rising sun less joyously than usual. The cattle in the field showed signs of uneasiness and fear. Blacker grows the cloud; thicker and heavier the air. Lightnings play about the mountain summit. Ever and anon a heavy peal of thunder seems to shake the very hills, rolling and reverberating among the surrounding peaks, till finally it is lost far up the lake. The birds hush their songs. Passers in the street hurry to reach a place of shelter. Children are called in from their out-door sports. The streets of busy, money-making Sodom are deserted and hushed. All hearts dread they know not what.

Now the sun withdraws behind the darkened clouds, and hides its face from the impending calamity. Then suddenly a new and strange light illumines the darkened scene. From a neighboring peak there issues a column of smoke, and stones, and salty ashes, and lurid flame. The thunders are no longer lost in the far distance. The whole air is tremulous with their reverberating echoes. The lightning no longer comes and goes in flashes. The whole southern horizon is sheeted with flame. It seems no longer even to abide in the heavens. For lo! blue flames run to and fro across the fields, in strange intermixture, as though they were uplifted torches borne by devils joining in some fiendish dance below. Now these lurid lights leap up in sheets of flame toward the darkened heavens; now they burrow in the ground, throwing up showers of soil and stone, and making huge chasms in the solid earth. The husbandmen run affrighted from the fields to find a shelter in the city. Their wives and children flee from the falling cities for shelter to the fields. The solid earth trembles and reels. Houses and temples, sought for shelter, prove only tombs. From the chasms of the earth the flames, upleaping, devour whatever the earthquake leaves. The air is filled with a shower of falling ashes. It is all alive with flame. Filled with dismay, mothers call wildly for their children; children call piteously for their mothers; and wives and husbands seek each other, but in vain.

But hark! what sound was that? Neither the thunder of the heavens, nor the artillery of the mountains, nor the groanings of the convulsed earth. The sea! the sea!

For now the waters of the lake, uplifted from their bed, roll in upon the plain. Water and fire contend in terrible battle for the mastery. Over the blackened fields and ruined cities God spreads this veil of waters, that the earth may not see the destruction he hath wrought; while the thunders of heaven and earth, the hissing of the red-hot rocks as the waters overflow them, the crash of falling buildings, the screams of the affrighted, and the groans of the dying, mingle in a chorus more terrible, accompanying a scene more awful, than any the world hath ever witnessed, or shall ever witness, until that day when the whole heavens shall be rolled together as a scroll, and the whole earth shall melt with fervent heat.

*"And Abraham gat up early in the morning, \* \* \* and he looked toward Sodom and Gomorrah, and toward all the land of the plain, and beheld, and lo, the smoke of the country went up as the smoke of a furnace."*

The story of Sodom and Gomorrah epitomizes the Gospel. Every act in the great, the awful drama of life is here foreshadowed. The analogy is so perfect that we might almost be tempted to believe that this story is a prophetic allegory, did not nature itself witness its historic truthfulness.

The fertile plain contained, imbedded in its own soil, the elements of its own destruction. There is reason to believe the same is true of this world on which we live. A few years ago an unusually brilliant star was observed in a certain quarter of the heavens. At first it was thought to be a newly-discovered sun. More careful examination resulted in a different hypothesis. Its evanescent character indicated combustion. Its brilliancy was marked for a few hours—a few nights at most. Then it faded, and was gone. Astronomers believe that it was a burning world. Our own earth is a globe of living fire. Only a thin crust intervenes between us and this fearful interior. Ever and anon, in the rumbling earthquake or the sublime volcano, it gives us warning of its presence. These are themselves Gospel messengers. They say, if we would but hear them, Prepare to meet thy God. The intimations of science confirm those of revelation. "The heavens and the earth * * * are kept in store, reserved unto fire against the day of judgment and perdition of ungodly men."

What was true of Sodom and Gomorrah, what is true of the earth we live on, is true of the human soul. It contains within itself the instruments of its own punishment. There is a fearful significance in the solemn words of the apostle, "After thy hardness and impenitent heart treasurest up unto thyself wrath against the day of wrath." Men gather, with their own hands, the fuel to feed the flame that is not quenched. They nurture in their own bosoms the worm that dieth not. In habits formed, never to be broken; in words spoken, incapable of recall; in deeds committed, never to be forgotten; in a life wasted and cast away, that can never be made to bloom again, man prepares for himself his own deserved and inevitable chastisement. Son, remember!—to the soul who has spent its all in riotous living there can be no more awful condemnation.

Alas! to how many the divine word of warning is as an idle tale which they regard not. Lot still seems as one that mocks. The danger is imminent, but not apparent. Men slumber on the brink of death. Woe unto them that dare prophesy evil. It has always been so, and it will always be so till time shall be no more. Noah, warning of the flood; Lot, of the destroying fire; Jeremiah, of the approaching captivity; Christ, of the irreparable destruction of the cities by the Sea of Galilee and of Jerusalem, city of God, are all received with impatient scorn. America laughs at the prophecies of her wisest men, and the baptism of fire and blood takes her at last altogether by surprise. Oh you who hear with careless incredulity the cry, Flee as a bird to your mountain, take a lesson from the inculcations of the past. "Who hath ears to hear let him hear."

He that heeds the Gospel message must be ready to do as Lot did. He had neither time nor opportunity to save any thing but himself from the universal wreck. Houses, lands, property, position, honors, friends—all must be left behind. Every interest bound him fast to Sodom—every interest but one. All were offset by that fearful cry, "Escape for thy life." What ransom is too great to give for that? The conditions of the Gospel are not changed. The voice of Christ still is, "Whosoever he be of you that forsaketh not all that he hath, he can not be my disciple." It is no easier in the nineteenth century than in the first to serve both God and Mammon. The judgment which God visited upon Ananias and Sapphira is perpetually repeated.

The Church is full of dead Christians, struck down with spiritual death, because they have kept back part of the price—because they have not given all to Him who gave up all that he might ransom them from sin and death.

"Remember Lot's wife." How many a Galatian Christian has begun to run well, but has suffered hinderances to prevent the consummation of the race. How many a Pliable flounders a while in the slough of despond, then goes back to the city of Destruction. How many a gladiator enters the lists, but shirks the battle. How many a laborer puts his hand to the plow, and then turns back. How many a soul, startled by the cry, Escape for thy life, commences to flee, then stops, wavers, hesitates, and suffers the incrustations of worldliness to gather over him, and turn him from a living witness of the power of God's grace into a fearful monument of the danger of a worldly spirit and a divided service. If to the impenitent the story of Sodom and Gomorrah is full of warning, to the hesitating, laggard Christian the story of Lot's wife is one of no less solemn significance.

Reader, if you are out of Christ you are living in the city of Destruction. There is but a hand's-breadth between you and death. But there is deliverance. The mountain of refuge is not far off. A voice, sweeter than that of angels, and far mightier to save, cries out to you, Escape for thy life; look not behind thee; escape to the mountain, lest thou be consumed. It is the voice of the Son of God. The irreparable past he effaces with his blood. The wasted life he makes to bloom again. "This is a faithful saying, and worthy of all acceptation, that Christ Jesus came into the world to *save* sinners"—not to teach, not to govern, but to save. For he comes not as a pilot to give safe voyage to vessels yet whole and strong; but to those already lying on the rocks and beaten in the angry surf, threatened every moment with engulfment, he comes, to succor, to rescue, to save. There is death in delay. There is safety only in the Savior's arms. "Haste thee; escape thither."

> "Haste, traveler, haste! the night comes on,
> And many a shining hour is gone;
> The storm is gathering in the west,
> And thou art far from home and rest:
>     Haste, traveler, haste!
>
> "The rising tempest sweeps the sky;
> The rains descend, the winds are high;
> The waters swell, and death and fear
> Beset thy path: no refuge near:
>     Haste, traveler, haste!
>
> "Haste, while a shelter you may gain—
> A covert from the wind and rain—
> A hiding-place, a rest, a home—
> A refuge from the wrath to come:
>     Haste, traveler, haste!
>
> "Then linger not in all the plain;
> Flee for thy life, the mountain gain;
> Look not behind; make no delay;
> Oh, speed thee, speed thee on thy way!
>     Haste, traveler, haste!"

THE WANDERERS.

## II.

## WATER IN THE WILDERNESS.

A FRIGHTFUL desert. Low rounded hills of stone, strangely colored but treeless, losing themselves in the dim horizon of a barren and illimitable waste of sand. Waterless wadies, marking, with their deep gorges in the soft sandstone, places where the mountain torrents flowed a few weeks ago. A burning sun. A strange shimmering heat that seems to exhale from the scorched earth. No shade. No trees. Here and there the stunted retem, the only vegetation to be seen. Not even the cool shadow of a great rock. A dazzling brightness that shines not only from the oppressive sun, but is reflected from the polished rock and the yellow sands of the desert—a light and heat that parches the skin, fevers the brow, makes the eyes smart with intolerable burning. Far as the eye can reach this same scene repeated; no tent; no tree; no attainable shelter; no pathway; a trackless desert; no sign, far or near, of human life.

Into this desert two helpless beings, mother and son, have come to die.

A life of strange vicissitudes has been that of Hagar. She is an Egyptian by birth. She has the dark tresses, the coal-black eyes, the olive skin, the hot blood, the haughty pride, the impetuous passions of her people. She belongs to a dominant race, yet is a slave. Servitude goes hard with such. It has gone hard with Hagar, though her master has been more than kind to her.

He has been, in fact, her husband. To be childless is, in the Orient, to be accursed of God. On Abraham this curse rested. His wealth increased. His flocks, his herds, his slaves were multiplied. Kings were honored by his alliance. But his tent was solitary. The poorest menial in his camp was richer than he. No sparkling eyes laughed with new delight when they met his. No chubby arms reached out for him to take their owner. No childish lips cried Father to him. Even the wail of a babe would have been a solace. Oh, the lonely, solitary, darkened house that has not the light and the music of children in it, a garden with no flowers, a grove with no bird, heaven with no harp, no hymn. Sarah—true woman in this at least—felt the void even more keenly than her husband. The age was polygamous. The wife offered to her lord her favorite maid. Hagar was promoted from slave to second wife, no great promotion in the Orient; but it was too great for Hagar. She despised the wife whom she fancied she had supplanted. When maternal instincts whispered to her God's promise of a child, denied so long to Sarah, she made no attempt to conceal her exultant scorn. It was more than the proud and sensitive heart of Sarah could endure. The true wife reasserted herself. Hagar was deposed. She became again the maid of the mistress; suffered a little while in proud silence the petty revenge of her intolerant foe; then fled to this same wilderness. Perhaps she hoped to find her way back to Egypt; perhaps she only hoped to die.

Neither relief was granted her. She must battle bravely on. The mother in her soul recalled her to her duty. A voice, as the voice of an angel, met her in the desert, and bade her retrace her steps. "Return," it said to her, "to thy mistress, and submit thyself under her hands. Behold thou art with child, and shalt bear a son, and shalt call his name Ishmael; because the Lord hath heard thy affliction." It was a hard battle between the woman's pride and the mother's instinct. But the mother conquered the woman. Hagar went back to submit her proud neck again to the yoke of an intolerable bondage.

That well-side, where she fought out the battle of her life which made her the mother of a mighty nation, she never forgot. "Beer-lahai-roi," she called it—"the well of him that liveth and seeth me." Who ever forgets the place and the hour wherein he first meets God and submits his own proud will to the will of the Almighty?

Hagar never retook her lost position. She was always the maid of Sarah, never again the wife of Abraham. So fourteen years passed away. They were years of bitterness; bitterness to Sarah, because God had given to Hagar what he denied to her, a child; bitterness to Abraham, who loved his son, and Hagar for his son's sake, yet could guard them from the petty revenges of his jealous wife only by repressing his affection; bitterness to Hagar, who bore with the patience of pride the anomaly of her position, mother of Abraham's heir, slave of Abraham's wife.

For that Ishmael was Abraham's heir she never doubted. As the years rolled on this assurance became the conviction of the patriarch's household. Abraham no longer hoped for another son. Sarah laughed at the bare suggestion. In Ishmael the promises all centered. Upon Ishmael the almost regal splendor of the old patriarch's wealth would all devolve. He would become the father of a great nation. The mother might die a slave; what matter, so that the son lived a prince. All this was instilled into Ishmael's soul. He shared the haughty spirit of his mother. He caught her infectious hate.

When, therefore, at length, Isaac, the Child of Laughter, was born in Sarah's old age, it was a bitter blow to Ishmael, the Child of Affliction. Sarah, the Princess, received the wife's true coronation. Hagar, the Stranger, became a stranger, indeed, in Abraham's household. Such a disappointment sometimes humiliates, but oftener embitters pride. Ishmael looked on Isaac as one that had come to rob him of his heritage. Yet Isaac's right to that inheritance he denied. Ishmael was the elder. He still claimed, in the silence of his own proud heart, the elder son's portion. But even this last hope he was not permitted long to nourish. When the time of weaning came, Abraham publicly recognized the young babe as his heir, with all the pomp and ceremony which always in the Orient accompanies this event. The mother and son witnessed with hot, proud hearts the festivities in which they could not join. Hagar, educated in the slave's school, had learned to hide her scorn beneath a passionless exterior. The son made no effort to hide his. Had Sarah possessed any magnanimity of soul, she might well have afforded to grace her triumph with a generous forbearance. She saw fit to dishonor it by humiliating her rival. She demanded that Abraham cast out the child he still loved so tenderly, and the mother who had borne him. Hagar was too proud to remonstrate. She accepted the leathern bottle and the scanty stock of provisions which Abraham gave her. Wrestling with the agony of a disappointed ambition, a crucified pride, a broken heart, she entered a second time the wilderness of Beersheba.

Before, the hope of her maternity sustained her. Now, she brought her boy to die with her.

The nearest haven was Egypt. A trackless desert intervened. She had neither path nor guide. She soon missed her way. Dazed, bewildered, she wandered on, she knew not why nor whither, only fleeing from the horror of the past, only hoping for some rocky shelter, by whose protecting side she and her child might be entombed together by the drifting sands. The water in the bottle was soon exhausted. The boy, faint and footsore, could no longer follow, with laggard steps, his mother. His parched lips, his swollen eyes, his throbbing head, his bursting veins, his frame consumed with fever, all told that death was nigh. She half dragged, half carried him to the shade of a stunted bush, and laid him there. The sharp agony of his death-struggle she could not witness. She withdrew "as it were a bow-shot"—for she said, "Let me not see the death of the child." Then her pride gave way. She burst into a fit of passionate weeping, that turned into a piteous, despairing moan for help, with no help near.

No help near! Ah! God is always near. But God Hagar had forgotten. Perhaps, in the impiety of her despair, she disowned the God of Abraham and of Sarah.

Oh, mother! blind with tears and anguish, though thou hast forgotten God, God has not forgotten thee. Thy son is dying of thirst, and thou of a broken heart, while close beside thee, almost at thy feet, God has stored treasures of water for thy supply. Does no vision of Beer-lahai-roi rise out of the dim past to cheer thee? Does no echo of the angel voice repeat the message that need never fail in the hour of even intense despair, "Thou God seest me?"

Blessed be God for the faith of childhood. Blessed be his name for the fruits of a father's example, seemingly lost, but garnered in unexpected seasons. The despairing mother gives way to passionate grief. To the God of his father Ishmael turns his dimmed eyes, and whispers, with parched lips, his broken cry for help.

*"And God heard the voice of the lad; and the angel of God called to Hagar out of heaven, and said unto her, 'What aileth thee, Hagar? fear not; for God hath heard the voice of the lad where he is. Arise, lift up the lad, and hold him in thine hand; for I will make him a great nation.' And God opened her eyes, and she saw a well of water; and she went and filled the bottle with water, and gave the lad to drink."*

Romance depicts no scene more touching than this picture from real life—a mother laying down her only child to die close beside the spring of life-giving waters, which her eyes, blinded by tears, fail to see. Yet how often is this scene repeated. How often we, too, in the wilderness, despairing, lay our hopes, our ambitions, our loves, down to die, just in the place, just at the time which God has ordained for our succor. How often our eyes, like Hagar's, are holden that we can not see. How often our despair is the prelude to our deliverance. We are never forsaken. God never forgets. In the most frightful desert experiences, the spring Beer-lahai-roi, Thou God seest me, is always to be found. For this sublime truth that God ever loveth me—not the world only, but poor me in my individual poverty, and suffering, and want—is not only a restraint upon us in the moment of temptation, and an incentive in hours of spiritual sluggishness, it is the Christian's unfailing source of comfort. In hours of utter loneliness, in hours when heart-sick we cry out, No man cares for my soul, there comes a voice from the heaven above, as the voice of an angel, which says, "I will never leave thee nor forsake thee."

I have read somewhere a fairy tale of a certain Prince who was attended by two angels, a good one and a malicious one. This prince was bent upon pursuing a certain journey, the issue of which would be his destruction. At every step of his way he found his path miraculously impeded, and as miraculously opened for him. A lofty and precipitous mountain was planted in his way. A tunnel, cut without hands, suddenly appeared, and gave him free passage through. A yawning chasm was cleft in the earth. A roaring torrent, beating against the rocks below, forbade all attempts at passage. Even while he gazed upon it, a bridge suddenly leaped out of nothing, and spanned the abyss. So it is in life. Only it is our good *genie* that opens the way where hinderances seem to forbid all hope of farther progress, that tunnels the mountain and bridges the chasm which bars our journey. That good *genie* is our God. "When thou passest through the waters," saith He, "I will be with thee; and through the rivers they shall not overflow thee: when thou walkest through the fire thou shalt not be burned: neither shall the flame kindle upon thee. For I am the Lord thy God, the holy One of Israel, thy Savior."

Nay, more. Hagar was driven from her home to find her God. She seemed to be going away from all good influences. She seemed to have turned her back upon the God of Abraham. She was journeying to Egypt, the land of heathen worship. But it was in the desert, not in Canaan, that the God of Abraham was revealed to her; as it was in the hour of her despair and her exhaustion that her eyes were opened, and she saw the well near whose side she had lain down to die. It is often so with us. God inhabits no temple. He delights to surprise us with unexpected revelations of himself. He is found sometimes where Zacharias found him, in the Holy of Holies, before the altar. But quite as often he is found in desert places. And where God is, there is holy ground. Hagar had heard of him in Abraham's tent. But she found him for herself only at the well Beer-lahai-roi, and in the desert of Beersheba. Moses had learned of him in his mother's home. But he did not see Jehovah until, an exile from Egypt, he wandered lonely and an outcast in the desolate wilderness of Midian. Elijah had often communed with the God he served. But he first heard the still small voice of his King when, seemingly deserted of God, he fled for his life to that same desert, and, in utter desolation of spirit, prayed that he might die. Out of utter loneliness come generally new experiences of divine companionship. The angels strengthen us only after our agony in Gethsemane. Jacob receives his blessing only after a night of wrestling. The Israelites, redeemed from bondage, came, so soon as they had crossed the Red Sea, to the bitter waters of Marah. The Christian's first experiences are often those of trial. We cry out against the bitter cup. We can not drink of it. Into the waters of Marah Moses cast the tree the Lord showed him, and the waters were made sweet. The cross heals all woes. The sweetest waters the Christian ever drinks are the waters of Marah when God has sweetened them. Our best and brightest visions are in our night hours. In life, as in nature, the bright bow of God's promise is painted only on tears.

Be not disheartened, then, oh weeping Hagar, nor let thy weeping blind thee to God's presence and God's love. Thou art never alone. The way through the wilderness is the way to Beer-lahai-roi. The hour of thy despair is the hour of God's sweetest revelations. Thy very tears purify the atmosphere of thy soul, and give thee a clearer vision. God comes into the heart most readily when despair has driven out all earthly hopes and ambitions. He dismantles that he may occupy. There is peculiar meaning, which experience of sorrow alone can fully comprehend, in the sentence, "When my father and my mother forsake me, then will the Lord take me up." God is nearest the forsaken.

But what if Hagar had shut her ears to the voice of the angel, and her eyes to the divine revelation of life-giving water. To have died—died with succor close at hand—is any thing more sad? I remember to have read stories of mariners who have crossed the deep in safety only to be wrecked within sight of their cottage lights, and to have their bodies beaten upon the jagged rocks by the cruel waves before their very door. I remember to have read stories of travelers lost in Alpine snows, and lying down to die within a few rods of the sheltering roof and warm fires of St. Bernard monastery. How often is this experience repeated. How many, many needless deaths there are. To how many a Hagar dying in the wilderness the voice of God's angel cries out in vain, "Turn ye, turn ye, for why will ye die."

The world is at best a frightful desert. It is full of bright flowers, and delightful shade, and luscious fruit at first. But gradually these fade and disappear. The journey grows more barren at every step. Our stock of provisions is scanty at the best, and soon exhausted. All the water we can carry in the bottle is but little, and is quickly gone. Our pleasures, our ambitions, our hopes, even our earthly affections, can not supply us forever. When this stock is gone, what then? Alas! how many a pilgrim lies down to die ignorant of him who is the living water. The voice of God calls to him, but he hears it not. His eyes are blinded that he can not, will not see. He dies—dies of thirst, while the spring of living waters, close beside him, seems to murmur, "Ye will not come to me, that ye might have life." God grant to you, reader, if you are content with your scanty stock, speedy desolation, that may drive you to him who alone gives true life; if you are already desolate and well-nigh in despair, a revelation of him who is in this desert land of ours "a well of water springing up into everlasting life."

C

REBEKAH AT THE WELL.

## III.

## ELIEZER'S PRAYER.

NEARLY forty years had elapsed since Hagar and Ishmael fled into the wilderness of Beersheba. To Abraham both were as dead. The promise of God, "The land which thou seest to thee will I give it, and to thy seed forever," was still unfulfilled. For nearly a hundred years Abraham had patiently awaited its fulfillment, and still he was a pilgrim and a stranger. Still "by faith he sojourned in the land of promise, as in a strange country, dwelling in tabernacles." From north to south, from east to west of all this goodly land, he owned naught but the grave of Machpelah. There his wife lay buried. There ere long he was to lie down beside her. And yet his faith waxed not faint. He still firmly believed that his seed should inherit the land in which he owned nothing but a grave. This glorious expectancy he would leave to Isaac. He had little else to leave.

The bond that united Sarah and the child of her old age was no ordinary one. Three years had passed since her death, and Isaac still was not comforted. Tender rather than strong-hearted, submissive rather than self-reliant, he still mourned as on the day when he stood with his father beside her rock-hewn grave. The light of his life had gone out. He was no longer a Child of Laughter. His hopes, ambitions, young affections lay in that grave where Sarah slept. He had no heart to think of marriage, even had Oriental etiquette permitted him to seek for himself a bride. But it did not. In the East no flowery path of pleasant courtship leads to the altar whereon love sacrifices. The marriage is a contract between families. Often the bride and groom do not even see each other till the wedding feast. This perhaps partly explains an ancient Jewish usage which fixed on Wednesday as the wedding-day. For, reasoned the Rabbis, the Sanhedrim meets on Thursday, and thus affords the husband an opportunity of presenting to the court without delay any complaint he may have to bring against his bride.

Abraham was the first to arouse himself from this stupor of grief. Oriental clans are separated by the same feeling of animosity which prevails among Indian tribes. They seldom intermarry. Abraham would fain seek for Isaac a wife from his own country and his own kindred. Religious considerations intensified this desire. Idolatry was universal. But in his father's household there was at least some knowledge of the true God. Ishmael had married a wife from the land of Egypt. Isaac should not be permitted thus to forget the God of his father. It is said that some one, surprised at the serenity of William of Orange in the disastrous days of the Netherlands, asked him, "Have you some secret alliance?" "Yes," was the reply, "with the King of kings; no other." This was the only alliance for which Abraham cared. Whatever else his son's wife inherited was matter of indifference to him so that she inherited faith in the God he followed.

Abraham had neither the energy nor the strength to undertake himself the task of selecting a wife for his only son. The journey to Mesopotamia was long, difficult, perhaps not wholly free from danger. He would not send Isaac. Desolate, lonely, the bereaved father could not suffer his only son to leave his side. But in his encampment was an old and trusty servant. For many years Eliezer had been the steward of Abraham's household. He was more like an elder son than like a servant. In earlier days the patriarch had purposed to adopt him, and make him his heir. Between such a life-long servant and the children of the household there grew up a peculiar and tender feeling, such as in our more mercenary age we can not easily understand. The feeling of the old slave-nurse for the white children she has tended helps to interpret it. This Eliezer Abraham summoned to his side. He commissioned him to go back to Mesopotamia, there to find from the patriarch's kindred a wife for the patriarch's son. He administered to him a solemn oath: "I will make thee swear by the Lord, the God of heaven, and the God of the earth, that thou shalt not take a wife unto my son of the daughters of the Canaanites among whom I dwell; but thou shalt go unto my country, and to my kindred, and take a wife unto my son Isaac."

Eliezer hesitated. He foresaw difficulties. What if the woman he selected would not come, a very probable and very perplexing contingency. Should he then come back for Isaac? No. On no account should Isaac leave the land which Jehovah had promised to him. If the chosen bride would not come, then Eliezer's duty was done. But she would come. "The Lord God of heaven," said Abraham, "shall send his angel before thee, and thou shalt take a wife unto my son from thence." The old man's faith was inspiring. Eliezer made the solemn promise. With his long caravan, laden with bridal presents, he started upon his singular journey, to select, in an unknown land and from the midst of strangers, a wife for his master's only son. A peculiar embassage—a perplexing one, too, we should say.

As he drew toward his journey's end, and the walls of the city of Nahor appeared in the distance through the golden twilight of the setting sun, his perplexity increased. He was not versed in that skepticism, borrowed of Aristotle, which denies that God attends to human wants. He knew nothing of that feeling which induced the Cretans to erect a statue of Jove without ears, because they thought it derogatory to the deity to suppose that he could hear the cry of humanity. In a few simple words he asked the God of Abraham to guide him. At the same time he proposed to himself a simple expedient, by which he would govern himself in the selection of Isaac's bride. As the breeze of evening abates something of the intolerable heat of the dry, hot climate of the East, the women gather at the public wells, which generally are dug just outside the city walls, and draw the water for their respective homes. Eliezer resolved, as the maidens came to the well, where he was resting, to ask of them a drink of water. This any one would readily give him. But if any one should do more, and offer to draw for his camels also, he would conclude she would make a good wife. The camel is a great drinker. To draw for ten is no easy task. The woman who would undertake it must needs have good health and strength, as well as boundless good-nature.

He had hardly finished his prayer when a young woman drew near the well with her pitcher in hand. Her beauty impressed the old servant the moment he looked upon her. We can imagine with what a beating heart he preferred his simple request for the drink of water. She complied at once. As soon as he had finished drinking, she proposed to water his camels. Without waiting for an answer, she poured the contents of her pitcher into the stone trough, which is the almost universal accompaniment of an Eastern well, and ran down the steps for another pitcherful. She did not cease drawing till the camels were all supplied. The quickness of God's answer amazed the simple-hearted servant. He seems to have proposed the test to himself with no real expectation it would succeed. What now to make of it that it had succeeded so well and so speedily he did not know. However, his quick intuition of woman's nature did not desert him. He said nothing of his errand. When Rebekah's task was ended, he begged her to accept from him what the woman of the Orient accounts the most valuable of all gifts—and perhaps the woman of the Orient is not so unlike her sisters, after all —some very rich and costly jewelry. At the same time he asked her name, and whether he could lodge at her father's house that night. To his new surprise he found he had fallen—by chance, as a modern historian would say—on a cousin of Isaac's. Bewildered by this succession of surprises, and wondering what the end would be, he waited while she ran home to show her jewels and tell of her adventure.

The rest is soon told. Laban's miserly soul was even more delighted with the golden gifts than was his sister. He thought that they could not have too much of guests who paid so well for hospitality, and ran out to the well to bring Eliezer back with him. But the trusty old servant would not so much as eat a meal till his business was done. He told his story, who he was, whence he came, his master's name, his errand, his prayer at the well, and God's answer to it. He ended by preferring his request for the hand of the maiden, whose turn it now was to be bewildered. Laban very piously submitted to the Lord's will. "The thing proceedeth from the Lord," said he. "Let her be thy master's son's wife as the Lord hath spoken." I fancy that the sight of the ten camels, and the packs they carried, quickened his piety somewhat; and his submission was rendered easier when he saw them unpacked, and "the servant brought forth jewels of silver, and jewels of gold, and raiment," and gave them with such profusion of generosity to Rebekah, and all the members of her household. For an old miser was Laban, and a cheat besides, who a few years after drove a hard bargain with his sister's son, when he was in love with Rachel, and, after making him work seven years for his prospective wife, succeeded in doubling his term of service by a scandalous trick on the unwary youth.

As to Eliezer, he was too impatient to get home again with his prize to wait for the delays which Oriental etiquette prescribed. Rebekah was of one mind with him. So it could not have been long after, when, as Isaac, in a quiet, thoughtful mood, was walking by himself at eventide to meditate, he saw a caravan approaching, and the wife whom Eliezer had brought back with him alight to meet her lord. A beautiful woman she was, and from the first Isaac was well pleased with the old servant's choice. The marriage was a true union of hearts. Perseverance mated to Cheerfulness makes a good match, and, if we interpret the Hebrew names, this was the match between Rebekah and Isaac. The wife took the dead mother's place. "And Isaac brought her into his mother Sarah's tent, and took Rebekah, and she became his wife; and he loved her; and Isaac was comforted after his mother's death."

The story of Isaac and Rebekah is not only interesting because it affords a striking illustration of the Oriental wedding customs of past ages, but also instructive, because it exemplifies both the power of prayer and the principles upon which it should be offered. Eliezer's commission, his journey, the scene at the well, the betrothal, the presents, the final consummation of the wedding, all carry us back to the most remote antiquity. The earnest wish of the bereaved patriarch that his only son may have a godly wife, his confidence in his tried and trusty servant, the oath he administers, Eliezer's faithful fulfillment of his trust, his confidence in Abraham's God, and his touching prayer when the critical moment arrives for action, all point up to him who offers to be our guide as he was the guide of Abraham and Eliezer.

There are many persons who feel a sort of timidity in coming to God in prayer with the difficulties and perplexities of their ordinary life. They are often told that in the presence of God they ought to put all worldly thoughts out of their mind. Actually to carry them to him seems a sort of profanation. The child very properly hesitates about bringing to his father, when he is busy with more important matters, questions about mere toys and sports. We feel perhaps as though God were concerned with affairs of such momentous import that it was a kind of intrusion to trouble him with the trivial details of our daily life.

But nothing is trivial to God which is of consequence to us. He is not so absorbed with the affairs of state that he can give no time or thought to the minor concerns of his children's life. Eliezer did not misjudge him in asking for aid in choosing Isaac's wife. Jacob did not misjudge him in asking deliverance from the threatened assault of Esau. David had no such hesitation when he said, "By my God have I leaped over a wall." Christ did not so interpret him when he said, "*Whatsoever* ye shall ask in my name that will I do." Whatever it is right to wish for it is right to pray for.

Nor has the day of God's counsel and guidance passed away. It is true the world has emerged from its childhood. It walks no longer in leading-strings. Humanity is thrown more, so to speak, on its own resources. But it is not orphaned. The oracles are not silent. Urim and Thummim are not departed from the temple; only now every heart is a temple to God. In every soul the oracle of God witnesseth. God did not cease to guide Israel when Moses died. Dreams, visions, heavenly voices, angel visitations have ceased. But God is not therefore silent. Eliezer neither heard an audible voice, nor saw a celestial vision. He expected no miracle. But God guided him no less than Moses, or Joshua, or Gideon. He who desires only to do God's will need never be long at a loss to know it. Events are his ministers, our teachers. Only for the most part we are like Balaam, bent on our plans, determined he shall guide us where we want to go. If we blunder, it is generally because, whatever we say with our lips, in our hearts we reverse Christ's prayer. Our real petition is, "Not as thou wilt, but as I will."

But trust in God does not take the place of common sense. I have read stories of devout Christians carrying their perplexities to God, then opening their Bible, and taking the first verse they lighted on as an indication of his will. But I never found in the Bible any authority for this use of it. It is no sibyl's book, no conjurer's cards. This was not Eliezer's way. He exercised his own best judgment, then asked God's blessing on it. Piety is a poor apology for intellectual laziness. Even in the littlest things God works out our salvation for us only when we work it out for ourselves, with the trembling and fear of eagerness. If the compass had been discovered in the days of Moses, Israel would never have seen the pillar of cloud and fire. It is said of Mr. Spurgeon, that when he was first applied to, to inaugurate an orphan asylum, by a lady who put into his hands several thousand pounds for the purpose, he hesitated. He perceived that it was a great undertaking, that it would require a large expenditure of money as well as of time. At last he devoted a day of fasting and prayer to the consideration of the subject. He resolved to undertake the enterprise only in case God should put into his hands a farther sum adequate to commence it. Within twenty-four hours he received by post from an unknown donor the required sum, to be appropriated by him, in his discretion, for Christ's cause. He accepted God's answer. The asylum was founded. It is thus God directs those who look to him for guidance. Life itself becomes luminous. Ways open in which God means that we shall walk. Ways are hedged up before us from which he would turn us aside.

Take counsel, then, Christian reader, from the story of Eliezer and the answer to his prayer. Carry your daily affairs to God. Ask his guidance in every emergency. Expect discoveries of his will. Let the promise of his help quicken all your faculties. Act for yourself energetically. Judge for yourself thoughtfully. Look unto God trustingly. Then will God both act and judge for you.

JOSEPH AND HIS BRETHREN.

## IV.

## JOSEPH'S STAFF.

IS every man the architect of his own fortunes? Or is there a " divinity that shapes our ends, rough hew them as we may?" Do we blindly stumble on where chance, or fate, or luck, or our own occasional glimpses of the future may guide us? Or is there one who is the Way—a Shepherd who leadeth those that trust in him "in the paths of righteousness for his name's sake?" The Bible gives to this question no more illustrious answer than it affords in the story of Joseph. That story is so marvelous in its transformations of fortune that it almost taxes our credulity. Yet it is so life-like in all its wonderful detail that it refutes skepticism. It is marvelous only because we see the completion of God's plan, which usually his providence hides from us.

Jacob seems to me the least attractive of the three patriarchs whom history always groups together. In him first appear the hard lines of that wily, selfish, calculating character which popular opinion attributes to his descendants. He inherits from his mother's family a mercenary disposition. It is intensified by his mother's teaching and example. The story of his dealings with Laban is the story of two cunning tricksters trying to overreach each other. He watches his opportunity to drive a hard bargain with Esau in his extremity. By an artifice, which no sophistry can palliate, he tricks him out of his father's blessing. When, twenty years later, he meets the brother, who through the long separation has been nursing his wrath, the same calculating nature still appears in his attempt to appease him by presents of cattle and camels. Even his piety takes at first the form of a sort of profitable venture. Listen to his first prayer: "*If* God will be with me, and will keep me in this way that I go, and will give me bread to eat and raiment to put on, so that I come again to my father's house in peace; *then* shall the Lord be my God." And this was the end of Jacob's dream, and the ladder, and the angels, and the vision of the Lord, and the promise of God to him and to his seed. Out upon such piety. This is but poor stuff for a soul when compared with Abraham, who was willing to leave country, kinsfolk, home, all, to be the friend of God; or with Joseph, who, a slave, a prisoner, an outcast in a foreign land, though dishonored because of his integrity, yet never disowned his God or sullied his conscience. Yet withal Jacob has the virtues of an industrious trader—energy, thrift, patience, perseverance; virtues which Joseph inherits from him, and of which he makes good use in time of exigency.

Real human nature is made up of curious contradictions. Strangely conflicting master-passions struggle for the victory. A bright gleam in the seemingly sordid soul of Jacob is his love for Rachel. A rare woman is she, a rare marriage is theirs—rare certainly in the Orient, where it is generally an alliance of families, not a union of hearts. There is the romance of real love curiously commingled with the story of trade and even trickery. Jacob finds his own wife, sets his heart upon her, earns her by his own labor, thinks no price too great to pay for her. When at last she is his, he clings to her with a love which finds almost no parallel in his age. His affection never wearies. It never loses the dew of its youth. When she dies he transfers his heart's love to her children, Joseph and Benjamin. When he at last lies down to die, it is with her name upon his lips, with the memory of her love brightening his past.

Oh, the bitter, bitter curse of polygamy—man's corruption of God's ordinance. Oh, the jealousies it engenders, the family feuds it produces, the hate, and bitterness, and shame it entails. The jealousy which Jacob's preference awakened between the sisters, Leah and Rachel, descended to their children. The sons of Leah hated the son of their mother's rival—hated him the more because the father's love for the wife became the inheritance of her child. They were not the ones patiently to brook fancied wrong. Simeon and Levi, at least, were men of hot passions, who hesitated not at wild and reckless deeds. So when the father, ignorant of their jealousy—or, at least, never dreaming of the lengths to which it might carry them—sent Joseph to the fields where they fed their flocks to inquire of their prosperity, unnatural as was their proposed crime, it was quite in keeping with what we know of their character and the turbulent times in which they lived, that they should conspire to murder him. How, by a stratagem, Reuben saved his brother's life—how Judah, who possessed something of his father's mercenary nature, succeeded in turning their purpose of revenge into profitable channels, by selling Joseph to one of those caravans of traders whose successors are to be seen to-day wending their way over the same road—how the brothers returned home with the coat, dipped in blood, summoning this silent but suborned witness to tell to their father the lie they had not the courage, with all their wickedness, to frame into words—and how Joseph himself was carried up to Egypt, and there sold to Potiphar, chief of executioners, the high sheriff of the kingdom—all this is too familiar to need scarce even this recalling here.

There were other reasons than those of birth for Jacob's partiality for Joseph. Wherever he went he made friends. There was something in his air and bearing that commanded confidence, ensured regard and even affection, and caused almost instantly the greatest trust to be reposed in him. He carried in his face, I fancy, as truly great men sometimes do, a sort of letter of credit, which said, more plainly than any letter could from any quarter, however influential, You can safely trust this man. Doubtless other slaves of Potiphar, seeing Joseph so quickly promoted to be steward—other prisoners, seeing him taken from the dungeon to be under-jailer—yea, all Egypt, seeing him called from the prison to be made prime minister in the kingdom—marveled at the Hebrew lad's "good luck." But the mystery of this "luck" we are able partly at least to solve. And one secret of it doubtless was a character so resolute for integrity that it uttered itself by his very mien, in a language which the dullest appreciated, though they might not clearly comprehend.

Then Joseph was somewhat of a fatalist. He never forgot those wonderful dreams of his youth, never forgot the bowing sheaves of wheat, and the adoring sun, and moon, and stars. He had faith in this dream as in a promise of his father's God, and faith therefore in himself and his future.

It is a poor sort of fatalism which makes men fold their hands and wait for fortune. Joseph's faith in God and his helpful Providence was of a very different sort. Because of it his ambition never lost its hope, nor his conscience its courage. He never despaired, never wavered. And there were eras in his life when he needed some such buttress to keep him from falling. If one might ever yield to distrust of God and despair for the future, this mere lad of seventeen might have done so, sold away from home, a slave in that land of intolerable bondage—Egypt. But Joseph's ambition did not desert him. A slave, he would still be such a slave as Egyptian task-master never had before. By the fidelity of his service he justified the confidence which his face demanded. Suddenly deprived of position, honor, every thing, and thrust, under false accusation, into that most hideous of loathsome and terrible abodes—an Egyptian dungeon—he goes to it with the same sublime and unfaltering calmness, refutes the falsehood by the same eloquent face, and becomes a prince even in prison. Lifted to the loftiest pinnacle which fortune, perhaps, ever bestowed upon a boy of plebeian parentage, he carries into the court of Pharaoh the same energy, the same foresight which had made him steward in the house of Potiphar and under-jailer in the prison of Egypt. He waits for no flood-tide to float him on to fortune; but he watches carefully to seize and use it well and wisely when it comes. In such fatalism there is no evil and much good.

Such a man, sustained by such a faith, is incapable of surprises. Joseph never loses his self-possession. Disaster never prostrates, prosperity never intoxicates. His calmness is something sublime, almost supernatural. He offers no defense when Potiphar's wife accuses him of the crime she herself had attempted. He receives the royal summons to the court as might a prince who hourly expected it, and takes time and thought to shave and dress that he may go in attire suitable for the royal presence. "*They* brought him *hastily* out of the dungeon;" but "*he* shaved himself, and changed his raiment."

Mark, too, what steadfastness of principle this unwavering faith in God and his word inspires in Joseph. He never flies false colors. By bitter experience he learns how false, as a worldly maxim, is the proverb, Honesty is the best policy. With him, however, honesty is a principle, no mere policy; and he never thinks of compromising it because it makes against him. "Behold my master wotteth not what is with me in the house, and he hath committed all that he hath to my hand; * * * how, then, can

I do this great wickedness, and sin against God?" A courtier, summoned to court, would have at least kept his religion in the background, remembering that the Church was mistress, and the priesthood the autocracy of Egypt. Joseph proclaims it in the first sentence he utters: "It is not in me; God shall give Pharaoh an answer of peace." Verily, faith so invincible, so calm yet so determined, so ready to act yet so patient to wait, deserves the rare reward that it received in Joseph's case. It would be difficult to find its parallel even among the remarkable lives that constitute so large a proportion of the Bible.

See Joseph, then, made prime minister over the richest, wisest, and most magnificent kingdom in the then known world. It is quite as often the minister as the monarch who governs the state. Pitt, not George the Third, was the real ruler of England. Richelieu, not Louis the Thirteenth, was the master of France. Joseph becomes, in fact, though not in name, absolute master in a realm whose government has always been that of unmitigated despotism. To maintain such a position for a quarter of a century is itself a test of greatness. To maintain it, a foreigner, over a nation that despises foreigners as the Egyptians did; to maintain it, a monotheist, over a nation whose idolatrous faith was so inwrought into the national life as it was in Egypt; to maintain it, executing a policy of heavy and burdensome taxation, not for present use but for future contingencies, this must have required a political sagacity such as only belongs to great genius. Cromwell, prime minister of Spain in the palmiest days of Jesuitism, would hardly involve a greater political and religious contradiction than Joseph the prime minister of Egypt.

The seven years of plenty, however, pass. The royal granaries are built. The taxes are levied. The stores of provisions for future needs are gathered. And the Hebrew slave, still a mere youth—for when a hundred years of age was the prime of life, he of thirty was but a stripling—is clothed in the white robes of regal state, wears the signet ring of Egypt's imperial despot, whose mark all Egypt recognize as the sign manual of unquestioned authority, rides in the royal chariot in state, second only to him whose servant he seems to be, whose master he really is, and is heralded wherever he goes by the courier, whose descendant still clears the way for royal personages through the narrow and crowded streets of Cairo.

At length comes the famine.

Oh, the horrors of an Egyptian famine. The pen falters in its attempt to portray what the pen of Dante and the pencil of Doré would scarce suffice adequately to illustrate. The clouds hold back their accustomed treasures from the distant hills where the Genius of the Waters takes its rise. Yearly this mother of life spreads itself generously over the fertile delta, which furnishes food for so many thousand mouths. For seven years it intermits its heretofore regular charity. Spring passes without seed-sowing; Summer without growths; Autumn without harvests. The rainless lands grow sere, and dry, and parched. All vegetation withers and dies. No winged commerce brings from more favored countries food for the starving. The cattle, unfed, grow lean, weak, sickly; stagger through a few months; then die. The poor soon consume the little store their own previous providence has accumulated. They eat carrion, corpses, dogs, dung, any thing. Whole villages are deserted. Emigrants flee from town to town in vain hope of succor, till their feeble limbs can carry them no longer, then drop down to die, unburied, uncoffined, and unknelled. The highway is strewed with the bleached bones of the dead, as though it had been the scene of some fearful battle or yet more fearful retreat. The people, crazed by the terrible and protracted calamity, prey upon one another. Little children are slain as sheep for the shambles. Kidnappers infest the streets of cities, and seize upon the unwary, lassoing them from upper-story windows, and killing them for food. The severest penalties are unable to check these unnatural crimes. The criminals are publicly burned alive. Their flesh is seized by the throng which gathers to witness their execution, and is devoured, thus ready roasted, with horrible greed.

Such is an Egyptian famine; not as the pen of romance, but as the pen of history portrays it. Twice in the Christian era this fearful calamity has fallen upon that ordinarily fertile land. We borrow our picture, almost our very words, from eye-witnesses of this incredible, unutterable horror, of which the Bible tells us only that "the land of Egypt, and all the land of Canaan, fainted by reason of the famine," and that the cry of the people came up to Joseph, "Give us bread, for why should we die in thy presence?"

That cry was heard. The Providence of God, and the

inspired foresight of Joseph alleviated, if it did not wholly prevent the public distress. The royal granaries were thrown open. The famished people were fed. Other lands had long been accustomed to flee in time of drought to Egypt, which, nourished at the breast of her mother, the mountain ranges of interior Africa, rarely knew hunger. The story of her marvelous supply traveled far and wide. "And all countries came into Egypt to Joseph for to buy corn; because that the famine was so sore in all lands." Among these travelers came at last the ten half-brothers of Joseph. One brother alone remained at home — Benjamin, the only other son of Rachel.

This was the only one Joseph wanted there. He nourished no revenge, but he felt no affection for his fratricidal brethren. The very sight of their faces was unutterably painful to him. He would fain bring Benjamin to Egypt to share his prosperity with him, and leave the would-be murderers to go their way. This at least seems to me to be the secret reason of his singular self-concealment, and that otherwise inexplicable stratagem with the money and the cup.

Nothing affords a more illustrious example of Joseph's power of self-control than his mastery of himself in the execution of his plan. No story of romance equals in dramatic interest the interviews between the brother and his betrayers. No elaborate word-painting could rival the power of the simple etching which the Bible gives us of these scenes. We stand in the court. We see the play of passion. We feel in our own hearts the tumultuous beating of the strong man's repressed emotion. The appearance of his brethren does not startle him out of his self-restraint. He notes at once that he is unrecognized. He preserves his disguise. "He made himself strange unto them, and spake roughly unto them." He compels them to tell him of the welfare of Jacob and Benjamin, yet asks no question that might betray him. He forces from them a reluctant promise to bring Benjamin with them when they return. The consciences of his brethren wring from them the tardy confession to each other, "We were verily guilty concerning our brother in that we saw the anguish of his soul when he besought us, and we would not hear." He makes as though he understood not their saying, and, for that purpose, carries on all his interview by an interpreter. Reuben's reproaches of his brethren bring before him the whole scene in the fields of Dothan. He still hides his feelings, going aside to weep the tears he can control no longer.

At length they depart. Patiently he waits for time to consummate his designs. When Benjamin at length appears in court, it is with difficulty he controls his long pent-up heart, yet still suffers himself to make no betraying utterance. He contrives the arrest of the one brother whom he loves, and orders the acquittal of all the rest. His plan is near its consummation. But when Judah, hot, passionate, bloody, yet with all the virtues as well as the vices of impetuous courage, pleads with impassioned eloquence, not for Benjamin, but for the aged and already thrice-stricken patriarch—when he depicts the sorrow of

Jacob at the loss of Joseph, and the unutterable agony which the loss of Benjamin will surely occasion him—when he finally offers himself a ransom in the young lad's place for the father's sake, Joseph can maintain his self-restraint no longer, and he breaks forth into uncontrollable weeping, while he makes himself known to his brethren, and attempts to assure their hearts by the half truth, "It was not you that sent me hither, but God; and he hath made me a father to Pharaoh, and lord of all his house."

It is not necessary for our purpose to trace the history of Joseph to its consummation. It is sufficient barely to recall the affecting meeting between the patriarch and his long-lost son; the interview between the father of the Prime Minister and his royal master; the solemn hour when the venerable Jacob gathered about his dying bed his family of children and grandchildren to give them a last blessing; and the farther prosperous administration of Joseph, until he, too, was gathered at a ripe old age to the grave of his fathers, and buried, in accordance with his last request, in the land which, after years of servitude and suffering, his descendants were to inherit as their own.

The story of Joseph is one of the most dramatic and romantic in sacred or profane history. It has not only been made the theme of many a sermon, song, and story in modern literature, traces of it are also to be found in modified forms in the Koran, in the canonical books of the Armenian Church, in the pages of Justin, even in the hieroglyphics and remains of Egypt. Its moral lies upon its surface. There is a virtue better than self-reliance. It is reliance upon God: reliance in times of adversity, calamity, distress; reliance which enables the soul to cry, "We are troubled on every side, yet not distressed; we are perplexed, but not in despair; persecuted, but not forsaken; cast down, but not destroyed:" a reliance which incites every faculty to a more healthful, because a more hopeful activity in times that call for action; which strengthens integrity in hours of bitterest temptation; which inspires the soul with invincible fidelity in the administration of every trust, " not with eye-service, as men-pleasers, but as the servants of Christ doing the will of God from the heart;" and which sustains the drooping courage in patient waiting upon God when hope long deferred maketh the heart sick.

Wearied and dispirited Christian, waiting with folded hands the redemption of the Lord, has not the story of Joseph's indomitable energy a lesson for thee? Rise. Fill to its full thy present sphere. It can not be lower than that of the Hebrew slave, a prisoner in an Egyptian dungeon. God helps those who help themselves. Rarely does he send his angel to give deliverance to the disciple who sleeps away the hours which should be spent in prayer and watching. Despairing Christian, bewildered in the storm that beats so pitilessly upon thee by thy doubts of God's goodness and care, has Joseph's story no lesson of hope for thee? Are thy misfortunes greater than those which for thirteen years followed the son of Rachel? Hast thou waited longer or more patiently than he the fruition of that love that to our eyes often seems long in ripening?

> Give to the winds thy fears.
>   Hope on; be undismayed.
> God hears thy sighs; God counts thy tears;
>   God shall lift up thy head.
>
> Through waves, and clouds, and storms
>   He gently clears thy way;
> Wait thou his time; so shall this night
>   Soon end in joyous day.

THE HEBREW FOUNDLING.

## V.

## THE GREAT QUESTION.

AMONG the names which redeem human nature from the dark pall of sin and shame which envelops the race, and give a true interpretation to the divine declaration that God made man in his own image, none is more illustrious than that of Moses. His name is brightest of all the stars that illumine the dark night which, from the days of the Garden of Eden to those of the Garden of Gethsemane, settled over the earth. Notwithstanding the lapse of three thousand years, it is still undimmed by time, which effaces so much that seems to its own age to be glorious, and buries in oblivion so much that is really ignominious. The founder of a great nation, his name will be held in lasting remembrance so long as the promise of God holds good, and the Hebrew race preserves, though scattered to the four quarters of the earth, its sacred records and its national identity. The founder, under God, of those principles of political economy which underlie every free state, his name will be more and more honored as those principles of liberty, equality, and fraternity, which were the foundation of the Hebrew commonwealth, are more generally recognized and adopted by the voice of mankind. More resplendent even than his inspired genius are that moral courage, that indomitable and unselfish purpose, and that manly yet humble piety, which are far too seldom united to a tenacious ambition and a powerful intellect. Deservedly honored as the greatest of all statesmen, he is yet more to be honored for those sentiments of commingled patriotism and piety, which lead him to reject a life of apparent glory, though real disgrace, for one of seeming ignominy, but real and undying glory.

Although Moses, alone of the heroes of the Old Testament, has written the record of his own life, we know very little of his childhood. The uncertain traditions of Jewish and heathen history furnish us with more ample material than his own pen. Unfortunately, these traditions are more ample than reliable, and afford little else than the ground-work for what is, after all, chiefly a conjectural biography. Combining, however, the history which his own pen has given us, the later Jewish beliefs as they are incorporated in the address of the martyr Stephen and in the anonymous Epistle to the Hebrews, the somewhat mythical traditions which Josephus has embodied in his romantic but unreliable history, and the fragmentary references to the great law-giver, which scholastic research has exhumed from the works of heathen authors, we are able to construct a tolerably complete and measurably accurate history of the birth, the early education, and the native character of the founder of Judaism.

Joseph's influence died with him. Following the Pharaoh whom he served was one, the records of whose reign have led the ablest Egyptologist to characterize him as " a superstitious sovereign, devoted to the priests, and a contemplative enthusiast." The priesthood resumed their old supremacy. The national prejudices of the Egyptians, against which Joseph had endeavored to guard his father's house, resumed their sway. Israel was reduced to the condition from which Joseph had emerged. The brethren of Joseph had sold him into slavery. Their descendants drank of the cup which they had prepared for him. The cruel punishments, the inhuman ill usage, which still characterizes the despotism of Egypt, remains, a mournful illustration of the simple statement of the Scripture, "Therefore they did set over them task-masters to afflict them with their burdens." The echo of "their cry by reason of their task-masters" is still to be heard in the melancholy antiphonal wail, sung in a weird chorus by the bands of workmen and workwomen on the banks of the Nile, "They starve us, they starve us, they beat us, they beat us." "But there's some one above, there's some one above, who will punish them well, who will punish them well." Nevertheless, despite ill usage, the Israelites multiplied rapidly. It seems to be the tendency of slavery to increase the number of the enslaved, and to diminish the number of the masters. To prevent the possibility of an insurrection, an edict was issued to slay all the male children. The people of God were threatened with extirpation by the sword of Osiris.

Such was the condition of Egypt, such the hopeless servitude of Israel, when Moses was born. His beauty at birth seems to have been somewhat remarkable. At all events, the mother thought so. She kept the child concealed until concealment was possible no longer. She then deposited him in a basket made of the papyrus, which grew in great quantities by the brink of the Nile. The Egyptian had a superstition that this papyrus was a protection against the crocodile — the river demon. Perhaps she shared this fancy. She set her daughter to watch what should become of the little waif. For herself, she could neither bear to witness his death, nor endure the suspense of utter ignorance of his fate.

Whether she contrived to put her babe where the Egyptian princess, coming for her customary bath, would find him, we are not told. Find him she did. Her woman's heart responded to the infant's helpless cry. She resolved to save it. Josephus attributes to the infant rare and precocious powers of discernment. He says it refused the breast of one or two Egyptians before Miriam ventured to propose sending for a Hebrew nurse. The suggestion, at all events, was made, and acceded to. Miriam called the babe's own mother. So the Providence of God gave back the child to its true, its natural guardian.

He grew up a boy of rare beauty — "was a goodly child," "was exceeding fair." Passers-by — so the Jewish legend goes — stopped to look upon him with wonder. Laborers rested from their toil to refresh themselves with a glance at his bright and beautiful face. The princess adopted him as her own. The Child of the Waters became an Egyptian prince. So soon as he was weaned he left his mother's arms. Every art was employed to make him forget his Hebrew origin, neutralize the influence of his Hebrew blood. His home was in the palace. Egyptian priests became his tutors. He possessed a mind as remarkable as his body, and rapidly acquired the learning of a kingdom not only then the most learned in the world, but that wherein later art and science received its first nourishment. For at the breast of Egypt modern civilization was nurtured. There is no reason to doubt that he was faithfully instructed in the precepts and principles of its religion. There is a probability that he was initiated into the higher orders of the priesthood. It is certain that he was intended to become a prince and a ruler. He acquired familiarity with the laws of Egypt and the principles of its jurisprudence. He not only acquainted himself with the civilization of his age, he added to it. "He learned arithmetic, geometry, astronomy, medicine, and music. He invented boats and engines for building—instruments of war and of hydraulics—hieroglyphics—division of lands." His military achievements outshone, in popular estimation, his intellectual attainments. He conducted with great success a campaign against the Ethiopians, and returned in triumph, doubtless the most popular man in the kingdom, despite his plebeian origin. This son of the unknown Hebrew mother, adopted into the royal family of Egypt, and connected by marriage with the court of Ethiopia, was second in the kingdom only to Pharaoh himself.

Yet he never forgot his birth, never dissociated himself from his own despised people. He was always thoroughly a Hebrew. When he was but a child—so the story runs—the king put upon his brow the royal diadem, in token that he ratified his adoption into the royal family. The child cast it contemptuously on the ground, and trampled on it with his feet. As he grew older, he rejected, with ill-concealed aversion, the religion which the priests of Egypt endeavored to inculcate, and worshiped by himself, without the temple walls, an unknown God. "He taught that the Egyptians were not right in likening the nature of God to beasts and cattle, nor yet the Africans, nor even the Greeks, in fashioning their gods in the form of men.. He held that this only was God—that which encompasses all of us, earth and sea; that which we call Heaven, and the Order of the world, and the Nature of things." So Strabo tells us. The priesthood are never tender of those who despise their authority or deny their teachings, and rarely scrupulous in their methods of getting rid of an adversary. More than once Moses almost miraculously escaped assassination. Nothing but the intervention of Thermutis, his adopted mother, prevented him from falling a prey to the anger of the king, who, if we are right in supposing him to be Rameses II., was not a monarch to brook insubordination in another, or to curb the passion of envy in himself.

Such is the story of Moses's life, as we gather it from the uncertain traditions of the past. It is now quite impossible to sift out the true from the false in those shadowy and somewhat mythical tales; but they indicate at least this much, that the youth gave promise of his future rare power, and that his impetuous temper, not yet chastened by forty years of solitude in the wilderness, and his uncompromising patriotism, which fitted him so well to become, later, the leader of his people, and the former of their national institutions, brought him into constant collision with as haughty, as powerful, and as unscrupulous a hierarchy as ever dishonored humanity, burdened a state, and disgraced the very name of religion. It is certain that fairer earthly prospects never allured a man of conscious power than invited Moses to cast in his lot with Egypt. It is certain that a sterner path of duty never frowned more forbiddingly, with less promise of honor or emolument, than that which called him to be true to the faith of his fathers and the people of his birth. Every argument by which trimmers and time-servers have been accustomed, in all ages, to justify their recreancy, addressed itself to him with peculiar potency. As an outcast, he could do nothing but suffer an unendurable slavery with the people whose lot he chose to make his own. As a prince, honored in Egyptian palaces, he might, at least, alleviate burdens which he would be in any event powerless to remove. By accepting his royal adoption he dishonored no name and sundered no ties, since none bound him to a people with whom practically he had never mingled. By rejecting it, he must seem indifferent to the ties which bound him to his adopted mother, to whom he owed position, education, life itself. Thus sentiments of almost filial affection, enforced by the apparent welfare of his own race, mingled with baser motives of concealed and unconscious self-interest in urging him to forget the land of his nativity, and become in truth a child of his royal patrons. Faith in God has perhaps never been more severely tested than it was in Moses's case. Uncompromising patriotism has perhaps never been more gloriously witnessed than by his choice, who "refused to be called the son of Pharaoh's daughter, * * * esteeming the reproach of Christ greater riches than the treasures in Egypt."

For it is quite certain that he was never recreant to his truly noble, but seemingly ignominious parentage. In the palace, as later in the wilderness, he was openly and avowedly a Hebrew in religion and in all his sympathies. It was no mischance, no sudden and impetuous act of an unregulated temper, that drove him from the throne, and wrested from his hand the sceptre. He *chose* "rather to suffer affliction with the people of God than to enjoy the pleasures of sin for a season." These stories of his rejecting the breast of an Egyptian nurse, of his trampling under foot the Egyptian crown, of his offering up his devotions outside the Egyptian temple, would have been told only of one who, almost from the cradle, rejected the land of his adoption, and clung to the land of his nativity.

At length, between the adopted prince and the Egyptian court there occurred an open rupture.

Moses had long borne in silence the wrongs of his people, which, keenly as he felt them, he was powerless to remedy or to avenge. Passion, long-schooled, grows sometimes overmastering. At length, one day, a peculiar injustice provoked his ire beyond control. He interfered, defended the Hebrew slave, slew the Egyptian master. The latter he buried beneath the sand. The Hebrew, perhaps, told the story of his deliverance. At all events, it became known. When, shortly after, Moses endeavored to pacificate a quarrel between two Hebrew brethren, one of them taunted him with his previous act. "Intendest thou," said he, "to kill me, as thou killedst the Egyptian?" Egypt was no longer safe. He had placed in the hands of the priesthood a weapon they would not be slow to turn against him. He fled the kingdom. The prince became again a peasant. The military leader of the Egyptian empire became a herdsman among the mountains of Midian.

It is not necessary to follow farther his strange fortunes. It is certain that when he fled from the royal court he had not the faintest anticipation of the future God had in store for him. When wandering through the trackless wilderness of the Sinaitic peninsula, he had no thought that God was preparing him to lead Israel through this same desert land. In abandoning the sceptre of one nation, he never imagined that he was to be the founder of another. He only knew that he would rather be a Hebrew herdsman than an Egyptian prince; that he preferred to follow God in the wilderness rather than to walk Godless in the most alluring path which luxury carpets, culture strews with flowers, and influence and honor brighten with their sunshine. When at length God called him to his allotted task, with the self-abnegation which belongs to true merit, he shrank from the undertaking. "Oh, my Lord," said he, "I am not eloquent, neither heretofore, nor since thou hast spoken unto thy servant; but I am slow of speech and of a slow tongue." "Oh, my Lord, send, I pray thee, by the hand of him whom thou wilt send."

Refusing the crown, Moses has received it. Mankind have already forgotten the name of the Egyptian monarch whose successor he might perhaps have become. Despite the royal works this Pharaoh accomplished at so great a cost, history has engraved his name so lightly that, effaced by time, scholarship spells it with difficulty, and pronounces it with uncertainty. The name of Moses, more enduring than the tables of stone on which, by divine command, the fundamental precepts of the Hebrew law were preserved, more enduring than even the awful mount where he met Jehovah and talked with him face to face, will live on in imperishable renown so long as humanity continues to honor the heroism of a true self-sacrifice. While the world stands, the story of Moses—his rejection of rank, purchasable only at the expense of fidelity to his own convictions, and his deliberate choice of a life of honorable obscurity, together with its marvelous and unexpected results—this will be told from generation to generation, a striking exemplification of the truth of Christ's paradox, "the last shall be first, and the first last."

When Joshua had crossed with Israel the Jordan, and had completed his campaign against the aborigines whom the Hebrews dispossessed, he gathered the people in the fertile and romantic valley which lies between Mounts Gerizim and Ebal; he rehearsed before them the wonders God had wrought for his people; he demanded that they then and there renew their allegiance to Jehovah, or then and there rescind their previous vows. "Choose you," said he, "this day whom ye will serve." When Elijah summoned the priests of Baal to the test, and built under the shadow of Mount Carmel the altar, and called down from heaven, to consume the sacrifice, the fire for which they had implored in vain, he set before the awe-stricken Israelites the claims of the true God and the false. "How long halt ye," cried he, "between two opinions?" To every person there comes such an hour, when, with unusual distinctness, the voice of God repeats this solemn adjuration, "Choose you this day whom ye will serve."

Such an hour was that when Mohammed stood on the mountain above Damascus, and, gazing on the glorious view, turned away from it with the words, "Man has but one paradise, and mine is fixed elsewhere." Such an hour was that when William of Orange resisted the specious arguments of Margaret, the persuasions of Berty, the pleadings of his own honest but misguided friend Egmont, and, breaking with the court party, whose honored representative he doubtless might have become, irrevocably committed himself to a life of self-sacrifice and a martyr's death, in loneliness so utter that he could write, "I am alone, with dangers menacing me on all sides, yet without one trusty friend to whom I can open my heart." Such a critical hour, too, was that when Napoleon proved himself unworthy of his genius, and incapable of the trust which the Providence of God seemed ready to repose in him — the hour when he sacrificed principle to policy, and, under a poor pretense of duty to the state, pronounced a decree by which he in vain attempted to sunder the tie which bound him to the only wife whom God or history will ever recognize as in truth his own. Life is full of such witnesses; illustrious examples of a noble choice and an unflinching integrity, or solemn warnings against an ignominious and a recreant decision.

The issue of the choice is not always what it was in the case of Moses. Religion is no secret road to preferment. Christ makes no promises of prosperity. He calls for volunteers. He offers no bounty-money. Nay, many a Moses dies, his life unrecorded save in the Lamb's book of Life, his name unknown save to Him who never forgets. "Verily, I say unto you, they have their reward," is no keen satire. It is a literal truth. The rugged path of duty leads often to the coronation of an undying fame. But it is not always so. Wisdom, Solomon tells us, has "length of days in her right hand, and in her left hand riches and honor." Nevertheless, she must be wooed and won for her own sake, not for that of her fortune. She often presents herself in the garb of poverty, and brings, in this life, only a dowry of suffering. It is no meaningless warning, that of the Master, "Which of you, intending to build a tower, sitteth not down first and *counteth the cost*, whether he hath sufficient to finish it."

The artist, Thomas Cole, has represented this truth upon canvas. A rocky, precipitous mountain divides the picture. Upon the right, a road leads through flowery meadows, by a smooth and delicious river, toward a prospect whose beauty, veiled in a golden haze, is more alluring than one could be which spoke more to the senses and less to the imagination. Upon the left, a rugged path leads up the mountain side. Clouds and darkness envelop it; while here and there, through rifts, are seen dark chasms, and a fierce torrent leaping over sharp and jagged rocks.

Before you, reader, lie these diverging paths. In your life there is, or has been, the solemn crisis-hour which determines all the future. To you God repeats the solemn adjuration, "Choose you this day whom ye will serve." Befog this question as you may, it is still the question of your life, on whose decision time and eternity depend. The question is not, indeed, always simple. But to every one the question comes. These diverging paths seem sometimes, at the outset, to be parallel to one another. But one is the path of duty. The other is the path of pleasure and preferment. One leads through the fertile plains of Egypt. The other seems to end in the wilderness of Paran. Mephistopheles does not usually acknowledge his name, as he did to Faust. But it is always the Prince of evil, however disguised, that makes the offer, "All these things will I give thee if thou wilt fall down and worship me." Christ points to the rugged road—his feet have marked it with his own blood—his Cross shines through the darkness and the clouds which overhang it—while his voice says, with tenderness, yet with divine authority, "Follow thou me." To follow him will cost something, may cost much. To pioneer that path cost him how great a sacrifice. But to turn away, what does that cost? honor, manliness, immortality, heaven, God. When selfishness and sense entice, be honest with yourself—count the cost. Before you reject the poverty of Israel's fellowship for even a princely inheritance in Egypt, ponder the question which Christ addresses to you, "What shall it profit a man if he gain the whole world and lose his own soul?"

> Why haltest thus, deluded heart,
>   Why waverest longer in thy choice?
> Is it so hard to choose the part
>   Offered by Heaven's entreating voice?
> Oh, look with clearer eyes again,
> Nor strive to enter in in vain.
>       Press on!
>
> Omnipotence is on your side,
>   And wisdom watches o'er your heads,
> And God himself will be your guide,
>   So ye but follow where he leads;
> How many, guided by his hand,
> Have reached ere now their native land.
>       Press on!

THE HUMBLED KING.

## VI.

## THE GREAT DELIVERANCE.

A MARVELOUS story is that Arabian legend, product of the wondrous Oriental imagination, of the fierce and deadly battle between two opposing genii, embodiments of good and evil—incarnations of the spirits of Ormuzd and Ahriman. A real truth is veiled in this weird story of singular self-sacrifice, whereby the guardian angel delivers the transformed and bewildered princess at the expense of her own life, consumed by the fatal fires with which she has been assailed by her foe who perishes with her. Thus the Savior of mankind delivers the race, bewitched by the arts of Satan and transformed from the image of God, yet dies himself in delivering us from sin and death. But more marvelous is the history which the pen of Moses has transcribed, of that strange and awful conflict between the God of Israel and the gods of Egypt, which resulted in the deliverance of the children of Jehovah from the despotism of their heathen task-masters. For that conflict was not merely one between the Hebrew race and the Egyptian race. It was not merely a trial of skill and strength between Moses and the priesthood. It was a waged battle between Jehovah and Osiris; the most marked and striking triumph of the true God over those which are no gods, which the Bible history affords. In that contest the very deities of Egypt were converted by the *fiat* of Jehovah into avengers of Israel's wrongs; and more than once the proud Egyptians were compelled to beseech the God of the Hebrews to undo the mischief which their own divinities were bringing upon them. Their religion was, as the religion of the Africans still is, a religion of fetichism. Whatever philosophy the learned of the realm may have entertained concerning the true nature of the invisible deity—and there is no polytheistic country so hopelessly degraded that God is left utterly without a witness in it—the common people "changed the glory of the incorruptible God into an image made like to corruptible man, and to birds, and four-footed beasts, and creeping things." They paid their devotions to the sacred waters of the Nile, to the cattle that grazed along its banks, to the frogs that croaked among its rushes. When, therefore, those waters turned to blood, the murrain destroyed those cattle, the frogs came forth in quantities so great as to be a burden intolerable to be borne, it seemed to Pharaoh and his superstitious people, if not to the more intelligent and therefore more criminal priesthood, that the very gods of the land had either turned against them, or were themselves cursed by a higher deity, whose decrees they were unable to resist.

It must have tried the courage of Elijah to face those four hundred and fifty priests of Baal, and trust his own life, and seemingly the cause of true religion, to a miraculous answer to his prayer for fire from heaven. It must

have required all the heroism of Daniel to go down, without tremor, into the den of wild beasts, and spend the long night-hours in their midst. Rare must have been the faith of the three Hebrew heroes if they did not tremble when the doors of the fiery furnace were opened, that they, bound hand foot, might be cast in. But it required faith no less invincible, courage no less calm and cool, for Moses to return, unarmed and apparently unprotected, to represent his people in the court from which he had exiled himself. Through all that strange experience, in which he contended with the Egyptian priesthood before the king, he was apparently at the mercy of the court. The supernatural protection vouchsafed by God to Daniel is not more marvelous than that which kept closed the mouths of the worse than wild beasts into whose lair Moses voluntarily entered. History affords few, if any, more striking contrasts of character than that which it portrays in this protracted interview between Moses, calm, patient, but resolute of purpose and unflinching in his pursuit of it, and the vacillating monarch, promising deliverance at the infliction of each new plague, and retracting it so soon as the plague was removed. We remember the lying pledges and broken vows of Charles the First of England, and Ferdinand the Seventh of Spain, and wonder not that, in the presence of such vacillation, even Moses should lose at last all patience, and should go out from Pharaoh "in a heat of anger." We see the flashing eye before which the ignominious monarch quails, when, to the royal threat—
"Take heed to thyself: see my face no more; for in that

day thou seest my face thou shalt die," Moses replies, with language more significant than any previous warning, "Thou hast spoken well; I will see thy face again no more."

In the history of nearly every nation there is a pivot-hour on which its destinies seem to centre—an hour to which all previous experiences conduct, and from which all subsequent experiences issue, and which remains fixed in the popular memory, and is ever after celebrated by song, by story, or by public festival. Such, in Jewish history, was the fourteenth day of Nisan.

When Moses returned to the land of Egypt from his sojourn in the land of Midian, Israel had already well-nigh forgotten the very name of their fathers' God. "Behold," said Moses, "when I come unto the children of Israel, and shall say unto them, 'The God of your fathers hath sent me unto you;' and they shall say to me, 'What is his name?' what shall I say unto them?" They had adopted the worship, if not the faith of the land of their bondage. At the very foot of Sinai they reinstated the golden calf of Egypt; nor was it until after nearly one thousand years of varied experiences of war and of captivity that idolatry ceased to be a national sin. They were scarcely more ready to listen to Moses than was Pharaoh himself. They complained bitterly of the first results of his intervention. "The Lord look upon you," said they, bitterly, "and judge; because ye have made our savour to be abhorred in the eyes of Pharaoh and in the eyes of his servants, to put a sword in their hands to slay us." They needed the lesson of the plagues scarcely less than Egypt itself—needed as much to learn to trust God as Pharaoh needed to learn to fear and obey.

But with every marvelous plague they had witnessed a no less marvelous protection. The murrain had smitten both man and beast in Egypt. The residents of Goshen had borne, in the midst of the disease, a charmed life. The hail had fallen in a fearful and devastating storm. The canopy of the Lord had shielded the fields of Goshen. The fearful simoom had brought up from the desert, in clouds of driving sand, a darkness such as could be felt. A mystic wall shielded the house of Israel from its invasion; and while Egypt lay enveloped in the supernatural darkness, "all the children of Israel had light in their dwellings." When, therefore, Moses at length commanded the people to make ready for their departure, we may reasonably assume that, although to sight their deliverance seemed no nearer, although Pharaoh showed no sign of relenting, and the tenacious priesthood no sign of fear, yet there were few Hebrews who did not obey the command of Moses, and prepare, with hearts curiously divided between hope and unbelief, for the emancipation for which they had waited so long, and with hope so often disappointed.

A strangely solemn night that must have been.

Egypt has already forgotten Moses's menace, "All the first-born in the land of Egypt shall die." Hitherto plague had followed close on plague. Now they have ceased. The priesthood seem to be victorious. The land has rest. No sickness gives warning of the approaching doom. No herald precedes the great king, saying, "Prepare to meet thy God." The Egyptians sleep.

But in the land of Goshen the darkness of the night witnesses, yet conceals, a strange scene of sleepless activity. In every household the lamb has been slain. On every lintel the significant blood has been struck. Within, the lights are burning, the table is set; in the silence of anxious expectancy the hurried meal is eaten. With girded loins, with sandaled feet, with beating hearts, Israel awaits it knows not what. And so the night wears slowly away.

Suddenly a wail arises on the still air of midnight. With the same mournful cry the inhabitant of Cairo still announces to his neighbor that death is in his household. But this is not the wail of a single stricken heart. It is echoed from house to house. It rises in a mournful funereal chorus of many commingled voices. Egypt sleeps no more. There are runnings to and fro, and priests and physicians are sent for, and vain attempts are made to succor the dying or resuscitate the dead. Angry curses, loud and deep, are muttered against the king, who has already withstood the importunities of the people, "How long shall this man be a snare unto us? Let the men go, that they may serve the Lord their God: knowest thou not yet that Egypt is destroyed?" Messengers hasten to the households of the Israelites to urge them to depart. The word at midnight comes from the court itself to Moses and Aaron, "Rise up, and get you forth from among my people, both ye and the children of Israel; and go, serve the Lord, as ye have said."

There is no delay—no need of any. Israel is already prepared. Slaves need but little preparation. Their flocks and herds are soon gathered. Their few clothes are quickly got together. The vacillating king has no time afforded him to retract his word again, were he ever so much inclined. The setting sun saw Israel in bonds. The rising sun witnesses every chain broken, and the people already well advanced in their journey toward the Red Sea.

"*And the people took their dough before it was leavened, their kneading-troughs being bound up in their clothes upon their shoulders. And the children of Israel did according to the word of Moses. * * * And the children of Israel journeyed from Rameses to Succoth, about six hundred thousand on foot that were men, beside children.*"

The memory of that night is still preserved by a national festival, which is to-day the most notable one in the whole Jewish calendar. In the mutations which time and expatriation have produced, the Paschal feast of modern Judaism bears only a remote resemblance to it in its original institution. But in the Holy Land, where manners and customs in the nineteenth century retain the form impressed upon them long before the opening of the Christian era, this very scene is still repeated, with the slain lamb, with the blood marking not only the lintel of the door, but the forehead of every participant, with the midnight meal of roasted meat and tasteless unleavened bread eaten standing, the loins girt about, and the feet shod with sandals. Still the children ask the meaning of this singular service. Still the Samaritan replies, in the very words which Moses dictated, "It is the sacrifice of the Lord's Passover, who passed over the houses of the children of Israel in Egypt, when he smote the Egyptians, and delivered our houses."

With different forms, and with different meaning, this festival still lives on in Christendom as in Judaism, the only remnant of that magnificent system of ceremonialism which the Cross has not destroyed. The temple, the altar, the living sacrifice, the flowing blood, the consecrated priesthood, have all passed away, never to be restored. The Paschal feast alone remains, perpetuated in a new form, to commemorate, for all mankind, a greater deliverance from a more galling servitude, by a sacrifice more terrible, into a freedom grander and more enduring.

Egypt still sleeps. The voice of God that warned in the Garden of Eden, "In the day that thou eatest thereof thou shalt surely die," is forgotten. The priests of Pharaoh still scornfully ask, "Where is the promise of his coming?" Still the justice of God whets the avenging sword. Still a careless world eats and drinks with the drunken, having no ears to hear the caution, "Watch, therefore; for ye know not what hour your Lord doth come."

Still it is true as of old, "Without shedding of blood is no remission." Not a virtuous life, nor a correct creed, nor a Hebrew parentage, nor a careful compliance with the as yet imperfect ritual which the unformed Jewish nation had received from the patriarchs, could bar the door against the angel of death. There was but one bolt he could not turn back; but one barrier he could not pass—the mark of blood upon the lintel and the posts. It is the Lamb slain from the foundation of the world that alone wards off the penalties of divine justice. Whoever hath accepted this sacrifice slain for him lives in the land of Goshen. Whoever has not is a dweller in the land of Egypt.

But it was not enough that the lamb was slain. The blood must be upon the lintel and the two side posts. The blood of the Lamb of God, which taketh away the sins of the world, must be applied to the heart. It must be evident in the life. The Israelite must put the mark of his nationality upon the outer casement of his house. He must designate himself publicly a member of a proscribed and despised race. The Christian must carry in his life the mark of his adoption. "Whosoever shall confess me before men, him shall the Son of Man also confess before the angels of God; but he that denieth me before men, shall be denied before the angels of God." A man may be a Christian, it is often said, and belong to no church. Doubtless. Thank God, there are not a few who cast out devils who follow not us. But no man can be a Christian and conceal his Christian faith, his Christian principles. There is no room in the discipleship for Joseph of Arimathea so long as he is a disciple "secretly for fear of the Jews." No man can wear the garb of Egypt and enjoy the protection of Israel.

For Israel's safety there was one condition—only one—faith. Of faith there was one sufficient evidence—only one—obedience. The Israelite must believe the warning and the promise—so far believe it as to slay the lamb, and put the blood-mark on the door. No skepticism that failed to keep him from that one act was fatal. No faith that fell short of that could save. Many a soul has trusted in the atoning blood of Jesus that could tell you nothing of the philosophy of the plan of salvation. Nay, despite much learned writing on that philosophy, it remains as insoluble a mystery as ever. Could Israel tell why the mark of blood should be efficacious to exorcise death? Could the poisoned Hebrew, writhing in death-agony, explain to you the hygienic principles upon which a look at a brazen serpent would cure him? Could Naaman advise you of the chemical principles in the Jordan which proved so efficacious to wash away leprosy? Could Lazarus offer you an intelligible interpretation of the mystery of his own inexplicable resurrection? Neither can philosophy explain how it is that "the blood of Jesus Christ his Son cleanseth us from all sin." What then? God forbid that I should refuse to arise from death when the voice of Christ cries, "Lazarus, come forth;" that I should refuse to bathe in the sacred river when the Great Prophet bids me "wash and be clean;" that I should refuse to look on Him who was made in the likeness of sinful flesh when the voice of divine mercy calls to me from the Cross, "Look unto me and be ye saved;" that I should refuse to accept the sacrifice of the Lamb of God, and apply to my own heart that precious blood which has given so many millions deliverance from the chains of sin and the fear of death when he bids me come unto him.

"We are saved by hope." Nevertheless, the promise of hope is a poor assurance of safety. Doubtless there were Hebrew mothers who, having fulfilled the divine command, waited in perfect peace the fulfillment of the divine promise. Doubtless there were other mothers who, having put the mark of blood upon the door-posts, pressed their children to their bosoms as never before, and waited through the long night, listening for the steps of the death-angel, with hearts in which hope and fear contended, in a wild and passionate struggle, for the mastery. Yet both were safe.

Oh, fearing, fainting Christian! who art never sure, whose faith sees the truths of God as the half-cured blind man saw "men as trees walking," in whose experience the promises of God are but vague and illy-trusted shadows, who art forever torturing thyself with thine own doubts—if thou hast heard the voice of Jesus, if thou hast accepted his love, and sought forgiveness and redemption in his blood, though the night be long, and the wail of humanity sore and bitter, and doubts and fears multiply, thou art safe. Such doubts torment, but never destroy. For you is written those remarkable, those precious words, "If we believe not, yet he abideth faithful; he can not deny himself."

The Paschal sacrifice was followed by a Paschal feast. The Lamb that was slain must also be eaten. "Except," says Christ, "ye eat the flesh of the Son of Man, and drink his blood, ye have no life in you." "If any man have not the spirit of Christ," says Paul, "he is none of his." It is

Christ, not only slain for us, it is Christ dwelling in us, bone of our bone, flesh of our flesh, who saves. Trope and figure are exhausted in the New Testament to exemplify this truth. We are the branches, he is the vine; we are the temple, he is the indwelling Spirit; we are travelers, he is the way; we are naked, he is the garment; we are soldiers, he is our armor. Only he is Christ's who follows the sacrifice with the feast; to whom Christ is daily imparted; who is able, at least in some measure, to say, "The life which I now live in the flesh I live by the faith of the Son of God, who loved me, and gave himself for me."

Like the Israelite, the true Christian partakes of this solemn feast with his loins girded, his shoes on his feet, his staff in his hand. It is not a feast of mere merry-making. It is a needful preparation for a pilgrimage. Religion is more than a creed, more than an experience, it is a life. One can hardly read the story of this midnight meal, taken in haste, and in expectancy of a summons to depart, without being reminded of the words of Jesus, "Let your loins be girded about and your lights burning, and ye yourselves like unto men that wait for their Lord."

The issue of all this strange scene, the great fact which its future repetition commemorated, was the emancipation of the Hebrew race. In a single night the shackles were struck from the wrists of six hundred thousand men. A nation was born in a day.

There are a great many persons whose idea of redemption seems to be that, in the far future, for Christ's sake, God will remit the penalty which, by our sins in this world, we have incurred.  Meanwhile, life goes on unchanged; there is no less power in temptation, no less attraction in the ways of sin, no new strength to resist, no divine inspirations, no supplanting of old desires with new and nobler aims.  There is to be seen in the print-stores of large towns and cities a popular picture entitled "The Rock of Ages."  In the midst of a yeasty sea there stands a cross of rock.  To it there clings, sole survivor of some fearful wreck, a woman, with the tenacious grasp of despair.  The waves leap up to sweep her away from her last shelter, while, from below, the hand of a demon of the sea seems seeking to grasp and drag her back.  And this is accepted as the type of trust in Christ.  This despair, clinging in the last wild hope to a barren rock, that can put forth no energy itself to save, this is offered, and widely accepted, as a picture of the Christian's refuge.

> "And is this all he meant when thus he spake,
>   'Come unto me?'
> Is there no deeper, more enduring rest
>   In him for thee?
> Is there no steadier light for thee in him?
>   Oh! come and see."

Is there no present, all-powerful Savior?  Does Christ's redemption wait in the future?  Is the Christian's hope like Israel's hope of Canaan while yet in the wilderness; like the soldier's hope of victory while the battle is still hot; like our hope of a much-loved friend's return still absent and long delaying; like our hope of spring in the midst of winter?

Nay, Christ comes to set us free from the law of sin and

death; to do what the law could not do; to preach deliverance to the captives; to set at liberty them that are bound. He comes to break the power of old habits, to destroy the embattlements of pride, to dissolve the chains of avarice, to conquer passion, to subdue appetite, to supplant vanity, to make of the soul "a new creature." He is called Jesus "because he saves his people *from their sins*." A thief is not saved because he is pardoned out of the Penitentiary. He is saved when he is reformed, and the thievish propensity is supplanted by honest aims. A sinner is not saved because he is delivered from the fear of death and hell. He is saved when the desire of sinning is taken away, and a new and nobler life is enkindled. This is the great deliverance which we celebrate in our Paschal feast.

Christ ransoms, Christ feeds, but, grandest truth of all, Christ frees—frees us from the fetters we have welded on our own wrists. To the cry of humanity, "Who shall deliver me from the body of this death?" "for the good that I would I do not; but the evil which I would not, that I do," the answer of thousands of voices, rising from every people, kindred, and tribe, in one sublime choral, is, Thanks be to God, through Jesus Christ our Lord. The true child of God, pardoned through the blood of Christ, fed upon the body of Christ, standing ready as a servant to fulfill the will of Christ, following without questioning the lead of Christ, though it conduct him to the very edge of the Red Sea, and seem to insure his destruction, beholds his pursuing sins overwhelmed and washed utterly away, and, able to do all things through Christ who strengtheneth him, sings henceforth, in exultant strains, "The Lord is my strength and song, and he is become my salvation." Forgiveness, food, freedom, these are the three great truths which the Paschal feast foreshadowed in the hour of its first institution, and which that Paschal feast, converted into a memorial of Christ's undying love, still teaches by its sacred emblems and its imperishable service.

MOSES STRIKING THE ROCK.

## VII.
## THE RIVEN ROCK.

THERE is doubtless danger of allegorizing too far in endeavoring to find spiritual meaning in all the incidents of the Old Testament. The Bible is not an allegory. The principles of interpretation which we employ in reading Bunyan's Pilgrim's Progress are not applicable to the books of Moses, or to the histories of the scribes and the prophets. They are what they purport to be—veritable history. But history itself is sometimes symbolical. This is peculiarly true of the Scriptures. There is not a little in the Old Testament which has a double meaning— one that lies upon the surface, and is discoverable by superficial reading; the other, which is hidden in trope and metaphor, and is discoverable only by a faith which has already been enlightened by the clear revelations of the New Testament. This we apprehend to be Paul's meaning when he says that a veil was upon the heart of the people, so that they could not understand when the writings of Moses were read. They did understand the letter. They were superstitiously scrupulous in regarding it. But they did not comprehend its prophetic and symbolic character. They understood its command of the Sabbath day, and were exceedingly strict in observing it. But they knew nothing of that unbroken rest, that perpetual Sabbath of the soul, which he who is in Christ enjoys, and of which the Jewish Sabbath was an emblematic promise. They understood the story of the creation, that in six days God made heaven and earth, and all that is in them. But of that new creation, wherein God makes of a chaotic and purposeless soul a new creature in Christ Jesus, they knew nothing. They understood, doubtless correctly, the history of the origin of the Paschal festival, and they never suffered the appointed time to pass without observing, with literal exactness, all the forms which had been observed on that first night when Israel stood sandaled and ready to depart, and ate the roasted lamb and the unleavened bread. But they did not seek to understand the real significance of a service whose prophecies were far grander than its reminiscences, and which foretold a deliverance immeasurably more sublime than that national deliverance which Israel celebrated. Of the Lamb slain from the foundations of the world they knew nothing. When Christ, risen from the dead, met the disciples on the road to Emmaus, utterly discomfited and in despair because of the crucifixion of their Lord and master, "Oh, fools," said he, "and slow of heart to believe all that the prophets have spoken. \* \* \* Ought not Christ to have suffered these things, and to enter into his glory." We should certainly be even more amenable to this charge if, despite his teaching, we failed to find in Moses and the prophets those foreshadowings of the suffering Savior which he chided them for passing by unnoticed.

Among the symbolic incidents of the Old Testament which, when they are thus read, interpret the New, there is none about which the Christian heart has more delighted to linger than about that of Moses striking the rock. The true interpretation of this fountain-rock in the wilderness is so plain, and its true significance has been so pointed out by the inspired writers themselves, that it is almost impossible to be blind to its meaning. "They drank of that spiritual Rock that followed them; and that Rock was Christ."

Israel had witnessed with increasing wonder the rising wrath of God against their oppressors, in plague following plague, until at length the cry of unutterable anguish at the bed of death in every Egyptian house had risen in one terrible funereal chorus, and Pharaoh had called for Moses in hot haste, and bade him and his people get out of the land lest all the inhabitants be stricken. They had stood in terror as the dusk of evening gathered about them, a nation of unarmed slaves, unfitted for war, encumbered with women and children, before them the waters of the Red Sea, upon their right the mountain crowding close to the shore, behind and to the left of them the hosts of Pharaoh, with horses and chariots, cutting off all possibility of retreat. They had seen with awe those waters separate; they had seen them mass themselves in walls on either side; they had marched through in long procession, with hearts in which dread of the massive waves, fear of their pursuing foes, and solemn awe at the majestic might of their divine protector were commingled in an experience than which it were impossible to conceive one more strangely, more awfully sublime; they had seen in the gray of the early dawn those waters released from the magic spell which enchained them; they had heard the cries of the terrified and despairing Egyptians mingling with the roar of the many waters hasting, at the word of God, to devour the foe who had so audaciously tempted him. Their scanty stock of provision had failed. God had fed them. They had come to a bitter spring of unpalatable water. God had sweetened it. They had found themselves in the midst of a trackless wilderness. God had been their guide in pillar of cloud by day and of fire by night. They daily witnessed wondrous manifestations of his power, and experienced wondrous evidences of his tender care. And still they doubted. Every new trial proved them false to him.

At length they encamped near the foot of the grand but frightful Sinaitic range. They were farther from the promised land than when they stood at the borders of the Red Sea. The rocky beds of the mountain streams were absolutely dry. Nothing is so dangerous for such a host, in such a wilderness, as to be without water. Hunger is more endurable than thirst. The passions of the populace are always fickle. They murmured against Moses. They complained of the God whose commands he professed to obey. Their dissatisfaction grew rapidly to serious proportions. Mob violence was threatened. The life of Moses was no longer safe. It is not easy to carry one's self with courage in the midst of such a panic. The faith of their inspired leader faltered. He felt the responsibility of this people. He knew not how to bear it. His prayer to God has almost the tone of reproach in it—"What shall I do unto this people? They be almost ready to stone me."

It almost seems as though God had purposely delayed that he might try the faith of Israel. He now intervened, and bade Moses take the rod which had already proved so efficacious; the rod at which the water had turned to blood, and the river had sent forth its throng of frogs, the dust had turned to lice, and the murrain had cursed the stricken cattle; the rod at whose beck the waters of the Red Sea had opened to give Israel deliverance, and had closed again to make for the Egyptians a grave; and with this he bade him strike the rock that frowned forbiddingly upon the camp which was gathered at its foot. Moses complied with the divine command. The rock opened its closed portals. From the frowning mass poured forth God's supply of abounding mercy. The thirsty and panic-stricken camp drank of the marvelous spring. And a new witness to God's loving care, a new rebuke to man's faithlessness, was added to the marvelous history of God's chosen people.

It is not merely a desert wilderness and the divine supply that gives to this incident its peculiar meaning. It is the fact that the rock, *smitten*, gave forth those treasures which lay hidden till the hand of man had struck it. It is Christ that saves, but Christ only as he is crucified.

The Rock of Ages gives to us the living waters, of which if a man drink he shall never thirst again, only as it is smitten by the hand of man. The spear of the soldier is the rod of Moses, at whose thrust there flows forth that stream of blood and water which is for the redemption of the whole Israel of God.

It needed no divine revelation to assure us that God loves. The language of nature and the experience of our own hearts are an adequate witness to this truth, so simple as to be almost self-evident. That which gives to the Bible revelation of God's character its peculiar significance is the fact that it reveals him one who affords the highest exemplification of Christ's precept, "Love your enemies, bless them that curse you, do good to them that hate you, and pray for them which despitefully use you and persecute you." The revelation of God's love, suffering for the sake of those that despise it, though so simple, is yet so august, so sublime, that our selfish hearts can not comprehend it, and our shallow philosophy obscures or denies it. Christ crucified is to-day as much as ever "unto the Jews a stumbling block, and unto the Greeks foolishness;" as much as ever the power and wisdom of God to those that comprehend it.

The true coronation of character is love. The true test of love is self-sacrifice. He knows not how to love who knows not how to suffer for love's sake. The love that costs nothing is worth—what it costs. The noblest names in history are those, the records of whose lives are written in their own blood. To suffer is grander than to do:

this has passed into a proverb. For illustrious lives we ransack, not palaces, but prisons. If we were to select the sublimest period in the American Revolution, it would not be the capture of Burgoyne or the surrender of Lord Cornwallis. Far more luminous with imperishable glory is that wintry march across New Jersey, when every mile was marked with blood from the naked feet of the half-clad soldiery, or that fearful encampment at Valley Forge, when, through the long wintry months, hope and faith waited on patience, and America proved her right to freedom by demonstrating her capability of suffering untold horrors for its sake. That Russian mother who threw, one after another, her children to the pursuing wolves, and escaped herself, may have loved her flock; but a true mother would have cast herself from the sled, and have rescued her little ones, by appeasing with her own body the appetite of her pursuers.

No type can adequately express the incomparable love of God. But we are not without types which illustrate the truth that the highest expression of love is self-sacrifice. Of self-sacrifice the Cross is the sublimest of all illustrations. It has cost God something to love. He attests the power of his love by the anguish of a riven heart. The Cross is the sublime symbol of a love which nothing can adequately interpret. The figures of the Bible are not to be subjected to a legal examination. It is a cold heart that comes to the Cross of Christ only to catechise him who hangs upon it. But certainly there is—one might almost say there can be—no higher manifestation of that love than that which is afforded by the sacrifice of a well-beloved son. The boy who dies on the field of battle suffers for his country far less than the mother who holds back the bursting tears, and vainly strives to conceal, beneath a calm exterior, her breaking heart, as she bids him God-speed when he leaves his home.

During the late Civil War, at the second call for volunteers, a young man of my flock left college and enlisted. He was the pride of his circle, the beloved of many friends, the reliance of his widowed mother. He was made adjutant of his regiment by the almost unanimous suffrage of his fellow-soldiers. He was their pride, and ours. Tearful and sad at heart, his mother gave him up to the service of God and his country. How we watched his subsequent history; how our hearts beat as we read of the costly valor of his regiment, and of him never dishonoring it. With what love his mother's heart followed him to Western Virginia, and to the Army of the Potomac, and through all that fearful campaign that culminated in the critical struggle at Gettysburg. Then followed long silence. Lines of travel were interrupted; mails were irregular; even the telegraph—broken, or too full of government dispatches—was mute. At length, one dread morning, came the short, crisp, telegraphic message, "Your son is mortally wounded. He begs his mother to come to him." Then followed the desolate journey, the hours of nursing in camp, the few last prayers, the hands of love closing the eyes of the dead, and the widowed mother came back with a heart broken, and to a home henceforth desolate. Alas! how many mothers learned, in a like experience of grief, the measure of God's love. For Christ lifts up this picture, and to every father and every mother that has stood weeping over the grave of the child he says, "Thy grief interprets God's love; for God *so* loved the world that he gave his only begotten Son, that whoso believeth in him should not perish, but have everlasting life." This verse, which Luther used to call the little Gospel, is, I think, the most sublimely significant text in the Bible. The most significant word in that text is the monosyllable *so*.

Yes, it is God smitten who saves. He not only does for us, he endures for us. It is this fact which makes it true that the "unspeakable gift" of God is Jesus Christ our Lord; that the highest glory of God, which gives earth a new radiance and heaven a "new song," is the Lamb slain from the foundation of the earth.

That lady who, turning away from the life of apparent ease and of refined culture which her parentage, her wealth, and her position combine to open to her, chooses to remain in Africa, consummating, in the loneliness of her widowhood, the work to which, in common with her husband, she consecrated her life for Christ's sake and the Gospel's, has given immeasurably more than any one can whose gifts, however generous, are all in money. Nothing that God has given can compare with this gift of himself. Nothing in this gift so adds to its lustre as that it is bestowed upon unappreciative hearts. "God commendeth his love to us in that while we were yet sinners Christ died for us." Jesus does but interpret the divine nature when, in answer to the nails driven through his quivering flesh, he utters the prayer of love, "Father, forgive them, for they know not what they do." Oh, miracle of love! From the riven rock flows the well-spring. The justice of God, smitten by the hand of man, becomes a fountain of mercy. The garden, the trial, and the cross call not down the thunderbolts of an avenging wrath. They supply a perishing people with the waters of life.

"God is love," says the apostle. We might almost transpose the apothegm, and say "Love is God." That is, it is love which renders him worthy of our worship. It is not the power which made the worlds and allotted them their courses; it is not the wisdom which orders all of life, and suffers not even the minutest detail to escape his notice; it is not even those æsthetic qualities, which have produced in divinely-created forms of beauty the types of all art and all architecture, that render God worthy " to receive power, and riches, and wisdom, and strength, and honor, and glory, and blessing." It is that his love is such that nothing seems to him too sacred to be sacrificed to the welfare of others. We sometimes look longingly for the day when in heaven we shall see the full glory of God, which now an impenetrable veil seems to hide from our vision. We need not wait. The glory of heaven is reflected from earth. It is not in the green fields, the perennial fruits, the crystal sea; it is not in the flashing domes, the golden streets, the pearly gates; it is not in flowers more beautiful, groves more Arcadian, music more celestial than earth knows that the glory of heaven consists. "The Lamb is the light thereof."

"The heavens declare the glory of God, and the firmament showeth his handywork," says David. But the cross of Christ, which David never saw, showeth his heart-work; and the song which the morning stars sang together in the hour of their birth is forgotten in that new song which the redeemed of the Lord sing unto the Lamb who hath bought them with his most precious blood.

> "Heaven is dull,
> Mine Ador, to man's earth. The light that burns
> In fluent, refluent motion,
> Unquenchably along the crystal ocean;
> The springing of the golden harps between
> The silver wings, in fountains of sweet sound—
> The winding, wandering music that returns
> Upon itself, exultingly self-bound
> In the great spheric round
> Of everlasting praises:
> The God-thoughts in our midst that intervene,
> Visibly flashing from the supreme throne
> Full in seraphic faces,
> Till each astonishes the other, grown
> More beautiful with glory and delight!
> My heaven! my home of heaven! my infinite
> Heaven-choirs! what are ye to this dust and death,
> This cloud, this cold, these tears, this falling breath,
> Where God's immortal love now issueth
> In this man's mortal woe?"

## VIII.

## THE FIERY SERPENTS AND THE BRAZEN SERPENT.

BETWEEN the Gulf of Suez on the west and the Gulf of Akabah on the east lies a vast peninsula, wild and picturesque in its scenery, uncultivated, and for the most part uninhabited. Not the ice-bound steppes of Siberia, nor the remote interior of Africa, nor the yet unexplored plains of Central China, present an appearance less attractive naturally to the common tourist. Yet thousands of pilgrims have crossed this inhospitable desert, and myriads of books, and letters, and pamphlets have been written descriptive of it; and it will stand famous to all time as the scene of the strange wandering of the Israelitish people from the land of their captivity to the land given them of God for their national home. Every site is marked and studied; every locality awakens a thousand strange imaginations by its sacred history or its legendary associations.

Not least interesting of all these monuments to God's wondrous power and yet more wondrous grace is Mount Hor, which, like a tower in a giant city, rises above the mountain range, of which it constitutes a most conspicuous feature—a permanent monument to Aaron, who lay down for his last sleep upon its summit. A wild, weird region is this, with great mountain peaks unclad with any verdure, but beautiful in their own strange and varied tints, like massive clouds at sunset; with wild gorges cut in their sides by mountain torrents; full of rushing water in the rainy season, but dry as the desert sand in the summer-time; with green oases of vegetation, that once were more frequent and more rich than now, but that at best were as islands in the midst of a sea of unclad rock. At the foot of this range of mountains lay Israel encamped. A long and weary journey their sins had led them. And though the air had grown fruitful at God's command, and the very dew had turned to manna—though the rocks had opened their barred and bolted doors at Moses's rod, and water had gushed out for their supply, yet it was not enough; and they spake against Moses and against their God, complaining even of his very mercies: " For there is no bread," they cry; "neither is there any water; and our soul loatheth this light bread."

Plenty begets forgetfulness of God, but grief brings us back to him.

Out of the mountain fastnesses, and from the shore of the now not distant gulf, there comes creeping up that most fatal and most dreaded foe of man, the insidious serpent. These glide every whither. They creep beneath the tents. They enter in through the apertures of the temporary booths. They glide noiselessly in upon the camps at night. No guard can protect against them; no watch warn of their coming; no weapon ordinarily suffices to slay them. Groundless complaints give place to well-grounded consternation. In every face sits dread enthroned. There is running to and fro; and the cries of the dying, and the bitterer cries of the living, wailing for the dead, resound through the night air. Herbs, and medicines, and all known healing agents are called for and applied—and all in vain. To the terror-stricken people it seems as though this valley was to be their burial-ground, and Aaron was to be accompanied to the land of spirits by the people unto whom he had ministered in life. Driven by fear, Israel, who could not be drawn by gratitude, cry unto God for pardon and for succor. They beseech the intercession of Moses: "We have sinned, for we have spoken against the Lord and against thee; pray unto the Lord that he take away the serpents from us."

God ever does for us more abundantly than we can ask or think. Israel implores only the destruction of the serpents. God undoes their poisonous work.

Into the midst of the camp comes the man of God, unfearing in the midst of calamity, because he that trusteth in God shall not be moved. To him, who has so often brought message of deliverance, the expectant people turn. At his command a brazen serpent, in the likeness of their dreaded foe, is lifted in the air, and borne, perhaps as a banner, from tent to tent. "Behold," he says, "God's gracious answer; for he is slow to anger, and great in mercy; he will not always chide, neither will he keep his anger forever. Look on this and live." And the dull eyes of the dying turn toward the sight; ebbing life begins to return; the sluggish blood renews its pulsations; the fevered brow grows cool; the unutterable anguish is alleviated; the burning thirst is quenched; from a thousand hearts there springs up the yet unuttered cry, "Oh life! life! life!" and soon from a thousand tents wells up a song of praise to God upon the evening air.

"*As Moses lifted up the serpent in the wilderness, even so must the Son of man be lifted up; that whosoever believeth in him should not perish, but have eternal life.*"

In a wilderness more wild than that of Akabah, in wanderings more hopeless than those of Israel, humanity struggles on toward its land of promise. It has never recovered from the bite of the serpent in Eden. The virus spreads, secretly, subtly, but surely, through the whole system. The dark background of history and experience is this—lost!

We are living in a country stricken with the plague. Disease is inwrought in the very fibres of our souls. It lurks in the very lintels of our doors. It is in the very foundation-stones of the earth on which we live. The soul bears witness to itself that it is lost to its true life. It aspires to something, it knows not what. The remembrance that in our Father's house is bread enough and to spare, steals sometimes in upon us with sweet invitations to return; reminiscences that are like music wafted over water in the summer evening. These very aspirations echo the word lost, while they point us to the "hope set before us."

I have read a legend of the early colonial days of America which runs in this wise. In the Indian wars which devastated the land, a village was overrun. Men, women, and children were butchered. Houses, barns, grain, every thing was consumed. For an hour the cries of the dying echoed among the hills, and the glare of the conflagration lighted up the clouds. Then all was over. One blue-eyed babe was spared. An honored chief took it under his protection. Perhaps he was more merciful than his companions. Perhaps a whim seized him to present it to his squaw. He carried it home. She nursed it, cared for it, trained it. The boy grew up to manhood. He knew no home but the wigwam, no life but the barbaric one of the woods, no parents but the dark-hued chieftain and his wife, no playmates but the red-skins of his adopted tribe. The son of a chieftain, he inherited his adopted father's place. He filled it with honor. His name was on all lips. His Anglo-Saxon blood asserted itself in the calm superiority which he felt, and which his comrades acknowledged. He was bravest of the brave. Judged by all the standards of the camp, he was deserving of the honors heaped upon him.

Yet within himself he felt a secret dissatisfaction—he knew not why; a strange yearning—he could not tell for what. Dim recollections of another face than that of his adopted mother, of another home than the wild one of the woods, stirred his soul in dreams and reveries. At length another war broke out between the nation of his birth and that of his adoption. He led his warriors to the conflict. It was long and hotly contested. Something of his own persistence he infused into the savage warriors, whose bravery is more impetuous than patient. But the arrow of the Indian was no match for the musket of the white man. The savages were forced to retire. They left their chieftain wounded, and seemingly dead upon the field.

There were Christian men in the settlement. They reconnoitred the woods to make sure that no savages still lurked there, then went out to succor the dying and to bury the dead. They were surprised to find a white face among the Indian host. His bow and his hatchet were still grasped in his hand. The heart was yet warm. They lifted him from the ground. They brought him tenderly to their home. They examined and dressed his wounds. They watched breathlessly his reviving pulsations. Their labors were rewarded with his life. And when at length the blue eyes opened and gazed about in wonder, and the lips, in Indian accents, asked, "Where am I?" they cried for very joy that one of their race was saved, not only from death, but from barbarism.

We are in a "far country." Judged by standards of the world we may be honorable among men, but he that lives without God is lost to his true life. The aspirations of his soul are silent witnesses to the forgotten home from which he has wandered—to the life of degradation he has adopted. Though he be a chieftain in his own tribe, he is yet lost. Blessed be God, who waits not till, wounded in the field of battle, we are left for dead; who waits not for us to arise and go to our Father, but who comes after us; who gives his only begotten Son to die for us; who heals the virus of the serpent by lifting up before us him who, though he knew no sin, has yet been made sin for us; who was wounded for our transgressions, and by whose stripes we are healed. Against the dark background of sin and suffering God lifts the luminous Cross of Christ. On the pall that envelops a dead humanity he emblazons, in letters of light, the word LIFE. In the ears of Israel, writhing in death-agonies, from which no human medicine can relieve them, a voice of one mightier than Moses cries, "Look unto me, all ye ends of the earth, and be saved, for I am God, and there is none else."

"What shall I render unto God for all his benefits toward me? I will *take* the cup of salvation and call upon the name of the Lord."

THE GLEANER.

## IX.
## THE BENEVOLENCE OF BOAZ.

NO book has done more to ennoble woman than the Bible. Other writings have contributed to ameliorate her condition. The Bible has elevated her character. It found her a menial, fulfilling the tasks, obedient to the beck, of her sovereign lord. It has made her a queen, rightfully sharing his throne, and wielding with him a God-given sceptre over the whole animate creation. It offers her, indeed, no fulsome flattery. It weaves no chaplet of pretty but poisonous praise for her brow. It makes no effort to conceal her faults. The woman of the Bible is no pure, heaven-descended angel, but a child of sin and sorrow, needing with us all the atoning blood of the Lamb for her ransom and redemption. The first sinner was a woman. Her hand unbolted the door through which sin and Satan entered to desolate the world. Among the last enemies whom Christ shall conquer is the mysterious scarlet woman, "the mother of harlots and abominations of the earth." But woman, if she is first in the work of death, is the first also in the work of redemption. The Son of God, whose lips never could speak to any earthly being the name of father, called Mary mother. She who unlocked the gates of hell has opened also, for a sin-cursed earth, the gates of heaven, and given through her Son free entrance to every child of Adam. And when the last enemy, which is Death, shall be destroyed, and the ransomed of the Lord shall come from every nation, kindred, and tribe to meet him, woman shall still be pre-eminently honored, and the most sacred of all earthly ties will be reflected in its heavenly prototype, for the Church, when at last it is presented faultless before God's throne of grace, "without spot, or wrinkle, or any such thing," shall be known throughout eternity as the bride, and heaven itself shall rejoice, with joy unspeakable and full of glory, in " the marriage of the Lamb."

Among the various types of woman's character which the Bible affords us—and nearly every type of womanly excellence is to be found within its pages, the singer, the preacher, the warrior, the ruler, and, highest and most excellent of all, the faithful wife and mother—two possess peculiar pre-eminence, because they have christened with their names the books which narrate the story of their lives. One of these books—an idyl, a poem in prose—is the story of a peasant-girl who became mother of kings. It is full of a quiet, rural charm which has invested the very name of Ruth with a peculiar tenderness. The other carries us among courts and court intrigues, in times of direst peril, and narrates plots and counter-plots as marvelous and exciting as imagination ever conceived. It is the story of a nation saved by the brave fidelity of a single faithful woman, who, by her queenly courage, has made the name of Esther truly regal through all time.

There is a period of Jewish history, between the occupation of Canaan under Joshua and the organization of the monarchy under Saul, which has been well called the middle ages of Judaism. It answers to the dark ages of European history and the colonial days of America. The people, possessing the faults and the virtues of a primitive age, not yet organized into a true nation, though not without the form of national institutions; occupying a new country imperfectly reclaimed from the aborigines, having every thing to do—land to till, cities and villages to construct, institutions to frame, government to organize—were almost absolutely without a literature, being as yet quite too busy in making a history to find any time to write one. It is in these times Ruth lived, and of these dim ages of antiquity, almost wholly hidden in the remote past, the simple story of her life gives us just glimpse enough to make us long for more.

One of those frightful famines which the peculiar climate of the Orient produces, and the marvelous improvidence of the people aggravates, drove from Canaan many of its inhabitants, among them one Elimelech and his wife Naomi, who fled across the Jordan valley, hoping to better their condition in the land of Moab. They gained nothing by their removal, however. Elimelech died soon after their emigration. Naomi's two sons married daughters of Moab, supported their mother a little while by their industry, then, one after the other, followed their father to the grave. The three widows were left desolate. Naomi, no longer bound by any ties to the country of her husband's adoption, returned to her native land. One of her daughters-in-law, Ruth, accompanied her. They were wretchedly poor. The ten years of sojourn in a foreign land seemed to Naomi full of bitterness. From comparative affluence she had fallen to abject poverty. "Call me not Naomi"—pleasant—said she; "call me Mara"—bitter—"for the Almighty hath dealt very bitterly with me."

The germ of those elaborate and often admirable provisions for the poor, which constitutes the glory—and, alas! by their inefficacy or their evil administration, often the shame—of Christendom, is to be found in the Mosaic legislation. Among other statutes was one which forbade the reaper from gleaning in his harvest or his vintage. The gleanings should be left for the poor and the strangers. This law, simple as it was, had some great advantages. It offered no premium on cunning idleness. The strong man could make better wages reaping than gleaning. It gave to the rich no chance for evasion. The poor gathered with their own hands the tax for their own support. It was the beginning of the barley-harvest when Ruth and Naomi entered Bethlehem. Hunger is a hard task-master, and they were absolutely empty-handed. Ruth offered to go and glean in the fields. Naomi was fain to consent.

The arrival of the bereaved wife and mother in Bethlehem made no little stir in the community, and the rumor of her return, and of the self-devotion of the daughter who accompanied her, ran very quickly through the little village, and came to the ears of Boaz, a distant kinsman. Her hap was to light upon his field, and he, an industrious farmer, who supervised in person the labors of his farm, found her there, following the reapers. He was touched by this new proof of her filial love, and her child-like trust in her mother's God, and bade her glean unfearing of interruption. He offered her no charity. What she took should be her right. But to his young men he added, quietly, the command, unknown to her, "Let her glean even among the sheaves, and reproach her not; and let fall also some of the handfuls of purpose for her, and leave them that she may glean them, and rebuke her not."

It is not difficult to imagine the scene in that field that afternoon: the young men sturdily plying their reaping-hooks; Ruth timidly following after, and looking up with glad and almost bewildered surprise as ever and anon she comes upon whole handfuls of grain lying in her path. Perhaps she thinks that these are very careless reapers, and almost doubts whether she ought to gather the grain they leave behind them. Perhaps she attributes her good fortune to the kindness of the young men, and occasionally repays their fancied munificence by a demure glance of her bright eyes. But she never once thinks of Boaz, who, a little apart, takes a greater delight in her bewilderment at what she thinks her "good luck," than he could have done in a more ostentatious mode of giving.

How the singular introduction of Ruth to Boaz led to a yet more singular courtship and marriage; how the daughter of Naomi became the wife of Boaz and the mother of a royal—yea, a more than royal—lineage, of whom was David, and, in years long after, born in a manger, in the same village of Bethlehem, great David's greater Son—all this is told with a detail which affords a striking illustration of the manner of that primitive age "when the judges judged." But to narrate it here would take us too far from our purpose, which is to indicate, in the story of Ruth and Boaz, a simple but beautiful illustration of a single truth.

The benevolence of Boaz exemplifies the aphorism of Christ, "Let not thy left hand know what thy right hand doeth." If, in after years, his young wife ever learned by whose direction she enjoyed her unexpected prosperity that summer afternoon, surely her gratitude and love must have been intensified by the delicacy with which the gift was bestowed. To give is as truly an art as to acquire; to give so as to seem not to give, this is the perfection of skill in benefaction. Munificent gifts, publicly bestowed and loudly heralded, do not constitute the most honorable, though they are the most honored form of benevolence. We do not sound a trumpet before us when we do our alms, but we advertise them afterward. We purchase titles of nobility in the Christian Church, and call it charity. We give as the shower gives, which heralds its coming with the thunder, pours out in one flood its multitudinous drops, and, after its charity is bestowed, hangs out the banner in the sky to call attention to its generous contribution. God gives as the dew gives, which silently, almost secretly, bathes the sleeping earth, and refreshes the thirsty flowers. We feel the freshness of the morning, and rejoice in the sparkle of its myriad diamonds, yet scarcely know whence the freshness and the beauty comes.

I think our hearts ought to be touched even more by the delicacy with which God bestows his gifts than by the munificence of those gifts themselves. He delights to hide himself, and watch, as it were, from his concealment our bewildered surprise at each new benefaction from our unknown benefactor. I like to think that he takes a peculiar pleasure in our very ignorance of him. Great handfuls of golden grain fall in our path. We stoop to gather them, bless our good fortune, and never think of the great and good Father who ordered them to be dropped before us. The farmer gathers his autumnal fruits into his bursting barns, and praises the fruitful year. Does he think of the God who gathered from the ocean the clouds that dropped fatness on his meadow-lands? The merchant rubs his hands with glee over his successful venture, and congratulates himself on the wisdom that planned, and the energy that executed it. Does he remember the God whose trade-winds, softly blowing, brought his ships from afar, and rendered possible his achieved success? The Italian, with many a song, treads out beneath his sunny skies the ripened vintage. Does he know that the hot sands of the seemingly fruitless Sahara, blowing across the Mediterranean waters, make his beloved Italy the land of the grape, or think who formed that furnace for Europe, and sent those winds laden with summer on their errand? When I read in philosophy and in poetry the praises of nature's wisdom and nature's beauty, I think of Ruth and the young men. Oh! fools and blind, not to know the Master whose servant nature is.

Even in the highest gifts of his infinite love he hides himself. By the shores of the Sea of Galilee stands the Son of God, surrounded by a throng whose eagerness for his words has led them far from home and shelter. He compassionates them, bids them sit down in companies upon the fresh grass—for it is early spring—then blesses and breaks the two small loaves and five little fishes. But he gives to the disciples to distribute. They are the almoners of his divine bounty. So still he distributes to perishing humanity the bread of life by the hands of his disciples. Father, mother, pastor, friend, from whose hands we have received the bread of life, these are but the young men who give the food their Master has provided. What thanks can ever compensate the kindly counsel of him who first pointed our burdened souls to that Cross at whose feet all burdens of sin and sorrow drop off and roll away? Yet he is but the almoner of God's bounty, the Joseph who gives from the granaries of the great King, the disciple who distributes the bread of life which Christ hath broken, one of the reapers whom God employs to drop in our path that divine food which is unto life eternal.

A little flower lay drooping on the ground under an August sun. For days there had been no rain. The earth was parched, and dry, and hard. The little flower had held up its open mouth for rain, but no rain had come. And now it was dying of thirst.

As thus it lay fainting, dying, a shadow passed over the sun. The air became darkened. Heavy thunder muttered its threatenings in the horizon. Lurid flashes of lightning chased each other across the sky. The sultry air became sultrier. The birds hushed their singing. The very leaves of the neighboring trees stood still for fear. At last two big drops fell at the root of the little flower. It was as if nature wept at its dying bed. A moment, and then the air was full of the descending rain-drops. They came as good Samaritans. They lifted up the dying flower, washed it, fed it, restored it to life. And when the sun broke through the retreating clouds again, two great tears glistened on the flower's little cheek—tears of gratitude and thankfulness.

Then the flower lifted up its voice and said, "Thank you, blessed rain-drops—good rain-drops—you have saved my life."

But the rain-drops answered, "Thank not us: thank the clouds; they sent us."

Then the flower lifted up its voice and said, "Thank you, blessed clouds—good clouds—you have saved my life."

But the clouds answered, "Thank not us: thank the sun, which saw you dying, and summoned us from the ocean; and the winds, which heard your plaintive sighing, and brought us hither for your relief."

Then the little flower turned to the wind, which bent down to earth and stopped for a moment to hear its words; and to the sun, which sent down its beams to receive the flower's message. "Thank you, blessed wind—good wind," said the little flower. "Thank you, blessed sun—good sun—you have saved my life."

"Thank not us," said the sun and the wind; "thank the good God. He saw you dying, he heard your sighing, he took pity on you. We, sun, and winds, and clouds, and falling rain-drops, are only the almoners of his bounty."

Then the flower, Christianly instructed, breathed forth a prayer of thanks to the great God. And the prayer went up, wafted on the wings of the wind, an odor of fragrance to the throne of the great, the only Giver.

## X.
## THE FORLORN HOPE OF ISRAEL.

IT is the theory of a certain school of medicine that it is the very nature of disease to provoke in the system a reaction which is itself the best cure, and that the only, or, at least, the chief office of medicine is to promote, if not to provoke, this reaction of nature against its foe. Whatever may be thought of this as a theory in therapeutics, it seems to hold good in the moral world. Out of corruption and death, and bred of it, issues a new life, as from the decay of the seed springs the new grain. Aaron Burr did more to render dueling odious than all the sermons which the pulpit ever produced. If slavery had not grown so arrogant, abolition never would have become popular. The absolute universality of drunkenness produced, by a necessary reaction, the pledge, which is almost unknown in countries where drinking is more common, but drunkenness more rare. To the shameful corruptions of an age which produced a Loyola and a Tetzel, the Church is indebted for Luther and Melancthon. If Catholicism had been less corrupt, Protestantism would never have attained its power. The insatiate avarice of the French nobility enkindled the French Revolution. The very fury of that revolution reacted in producing a new and firm, though still despotic government. If it had not been for Charles I., England would never have had a Cromwell and a Hampden. To the licentious Cavalier the world is indebted for the virtuous but too rigid Puritan. The power of primitive Christianity is partly owing to the strong reaction of the popular mind, at least of the more virtuous portion, against the degrading superstitions of the pagan idolatry. Paul would scarcely have been possible had there been no Gamaliel.

It was in an era of great national degradation and distress that the character of Gideon, Israel's great deliverer, was formed. The nation seemed, indeed, to be upon the very eve of utter extinction. There had never been an hour in the national history when they were wholly free from the incursions of the Bedouin Arabs, whose lawless descendants still roam the desert lands east of Palestine. But with loss of faith in God came loss of manly courage founded on it. The Israelite offered but feeble resistance to these increasing forays. At length Arabians, Amalekites, and Midianites made common cause against those whom they regarded as a common prey, if not as a common foe. Emboldened by success, they crossed the valley of the Jordan, and planted their encampments along the hill-sides of Manasseh and Ephraim. They waited each year till the fattening herds and ripening grain invited their incursions. Then, unresisted and unavenged, they swept through the whole land, from the Sea of Galilee to the gates of Gaza, like a host of locusts or a fierce consuming fire. They "left no sustenance for Israel, neither sheep, nor ox, nor ass." No less cruel than greedy, they were as ready to seize a stalwart young man for a slave, or a fair young maiden for a concubine, as the cattle or the standing grain for booty. The frightened Israelites, not daring to resist, indeed quite unable in their own strength to do so, fled to the mountain fastnesses. From the dens and caves, which later served the brigands of the Holy Land a refuge from the legions of the Cæsars, they witnessed in despair the despoiling of their homes. For seven years this operation had been repeated, till the land was far worse than famine-stricken. To the desperate people no choice seemed left but death from starvation in the mountains, or death from the Bedouin swords upon the plains. And still the warnings of Moses and Joshua were never brought to mind; still the worship of Baal and Ashtaroth supplanted that of Jehovah.

Such is the condition of the chosen people of God at the time when history introduces us to Gideon. His father's fields and herds have suffered in the universal devastation. In some hopeless attempt at defense, or more hopeless attempt at reprisal, his brethren have been captured, and in cold blood put to death for daring to defend their firesides from the invader. In solitude, this youngest son, left to be the only stay of his father's old age, is beating out by hand a little wheat saved from the remorseless Arab hordes. He has constructed a rude threshing-floor in one of those primitive wine-vats which Nature had provided in the cavernous hills of Palestine—an aperture in the limestone, half chasm, half cave—where, in Canaan's happier days, he had often pressed the grape with dancing feet and merry song. In like hiding-places, among the wadies of the wooded hills, the modern poverty-stricken peasant still conceals his grain from the lawless freebooters of the desert. Youngest of his father's family, Gideon has, nevertheless, a boy grown well on toward man's estate. With the pretense of humility, but in language which sounds like that of ill-concealed pride, he designates his family as poor in Manasseh, himself as least in his father's house. His father, nevertheless, would appear to be a man of some means as well as influence. He has erected, at his own expense, an altar to Baal, and put by the side of it one of those rude images of Ashtaroth, carved in wood, which witnesses at once to the degradation of Israel's worship and the licentiousness of Israel's manners. Gideon himself owns a retinue of slaves, and has already attained no little honor in his tribe, if, indeed, his past exploits have not made him known for a mighty man of valor throughout the nation. He is a man of courage, yet of caution; has not, in his despair, wholly lost all faith in God, yet gives himself up to bitter thoughts as he recalls the tales he loved to hear in his early youth of Israel's achievements, when Joshua led them, invincible, against these same barbarian hordes at whose feet they now are crouching. As he swings the flail in his rude threshing-floor, and wishes that he might thus beat the oppressors of his nation with an avenging arm, he mutters to himself, I fancy, almost the very words of later skepticism, "Where is the promise of his coming?" So employed, the very solitude of his labor breeding these bitter reflections, he is startled by a salutation close beside him, "The Lord is with thee, thou mighty man of valor." His answer is the utterance, in caustic irony, of his previous meditations, "If the Lord be with us, why then is all this befallen us? And where be all his miracles which our fathers told us of? * * * The Lord hath forsaken us, and delivered us into the hands of the Midianites." "Go in this thy might," replies the mysterious stranger, "and thou shalt save Israel from the hand of the Midianites." But the appeal enkindles no enthusiasm in Gideon. Like his prototype Moses, he begs to be excused. At length some faint idea that it is no ordinary man he talks with seems to dawn upon him. Perhaps he remembers the story of Abraham's heavenly visitors. He hastens away to fetch a kid and some unleavened cakes for his guest. He sets them out upon the rocky table—a primitive repast. But no sooner has he done so, than the Unknown touches them with his staff; the rock becomes an altar, fire leaps forth from it, and, while Gideon is transfixed to find his proffered food converted into a burnt-offering to the Lord, the angel departs as silently and mysteriously as he arrived. Gideon is left alone to accept this commission, so strangely conferred upon him, or to reject it as he will.

One thing is clear to him, that, though Israel has quite forgotten the Lord, the Lord has not forgotten Israel. Another, as he thinks more of it, is quite as clear, that, to have the help of the Lord in any future plans, the first step is a personal repentance of the sin of idolatry, and a personal recognition of the God whose right arm hath gotten them in the past their victories. This thought comes to him at night as he lies upon his bed, sleepless for thinking over the events of the day. With it comes an impulse to rise straightway and destroy the altar to Baal and the image of Ashtaroth which curse his father's grounds. He attributes this impulse to the God with whose angel messenger he has talked face to face. We may at least question whether our philosophy would not be wiser if it attributed to the same heavenly Counselor those similar surprises which come sometimes to us in our better moods as revelations from an unseen world. This voice of God he will obey—obey at once. So, without delay, he rises, summons ten of his most trusty servants, and, while the not distant city of Ophrah is still wrapped in sleep, casts down the heathen altar, cuts down the heathen idol—not the grove, as our English version improperly renders it—erects on this very spot a rude altar to the God of his fathers, and mingles with the light of early dawn the fires of his first true sacrifice. From this time forth his position is publicly taken, the position of the leader whom he so much admires: "As for me and my house, we will serve the Lord." In the name of the almost forgotten Jehovah he conducts henceforth his entire campaign.

The people, awaking to find their altar cast down and their goddess ruthlessly destroyed, demand, with angry imprecations, the death of the impious iconoclast. The bereaved father ingeniously interposes to save his sole surviving son. "Will ye plead for Baal?" he cries. "If he be a god, let him plead for himself." The argument is efficacious. It is the same as that which smote with such terrific force upon the Philistines in Ashdod, when, a century later, Dagon fell prostrate in his temple before the captured ark of God; the same which, during the reign of the Roman emperor Theodosius, converted the silent awe with which the heathen at first witnessed the destruction of their god at Alexandria into boisterous ridicule, when they perceived that he was unable to defend himself, and incited them to join with their Christian antagonists in immolating Serapis in his own temple. It is, in fact, an argument of universal application. Society may rightfully defend itself from threatened wrong, perhaps avenge wrongs committed; but it is neither the business of the state to maintain true religion nor to punish the false. God needs no defenders. He can plead for himself.

The wild fury of the people at Gideon's audacity reacts in an equally wild enthusiasm, enkindled by his courage. From demanding his head, they pass, by one of those transitions of popular feeling which are as inexplicable as they are common, to clamorously crowning him as their leader. His own clan of Abiezer gathers about him. His tribe of Manasseh answers to his trumpet-call. Heralds go out to the neighboring territories of Asher, Zebulon, and Naphthali. The time is really auspicious, though it seems to be the reverse. The very despair of the people nerves them with courage. From their hiding-places in the hills the volunteers flock to Gideon's camp. There gathers about him an army of thirty-two thousand men. The Midianites, too, hear this note of war. They concentrate their forces to prepare for the conflict. One hundred and twenty thousand strong, they encamp on the hills that overlook the plains of Esdraelon. So the elements gather for the storm.

Judged by ordinary military standards, Gideon's forces are quite inadequate for his purpose. His men are ill equipped, untrained, unused to war. They are to cope with a force four times as large, of Bedouins trained to war from childhood. No wonder that Gideon's faith falters. The already half-forgotten traditions are inadequate for such a crisis. He asks for some assurance of God's help. It is vouchsafed. He leaves a fleece of wool upon the ground. The dews saturate it though the earth is dry. This might be a chance. He begs leave to reverse the experiment. It is granted. Upon the following night the fleece alone is dry, the earth is wet with a heavy dew. It is a queer conceit that sees in this incident a symbolic interpretation of Gideon himself, "cool in the heat of all around, dry when all around were damped with fear." The history indicates nothing more than a purely artificial test of Gideon's own designing.

He has tried God. Now God will try him. The thirty-two thousand men who have gathered at his call are too few for Gideon. They are too many for God. The laws of Moses not only provided Israel with no standing army; they prescribed explicitly that the army should be composed of volunteers. On the eve of every campaign the officers were required to issue this proclamation to the people: "What man is there that is fearful and fainthearted? Let him go and return unto his house, lest his brethren's heart faint as well as his heart." Gideon is reminded of this law. He issues the required proclamation. The Israelites are encamped on the slope of Mount Gilboa. The valley of Jezreel lies between them and the heathen host. The sight of their foe in battle array is sufficient to dampen the military ardor of many of Gideon's raw recruits. A third of his little army avail themselves of his permission to retire. Still too many remain. Near their camp, a spring, welling up, sends forth a copious stream to add to the fertility of the adjoining plain. Ever since the hour of this encampment, it has been known as the Spring of Trembling. The soldiers are brought by divine command to this spring to drink. Some kneel down at the water's edge and drink from the running brook. Some dip up the water in their hand. The latter God selects for the campaign. There are but three hundred of them. The rest return to their tents to await the result.

That night, as darkness gathers over the camps of Israel and of Midian, and both hosts are wrapped in slumber, Gideon, accompanied only by his armor-bearer, creeps across the valley to the very edge of the heathen tents to reconnoitre. God has promised that he shall hear what will strengthen his courage. Stealthily he enters the heathen lines. He comes to one wakeful group. An Arab is telling to his fellows a dream. He has seen in his sleep a cake of barley tumble into the camp, roll down the hillside, and, smiting a tent—Josephus says the royal tent—bring it to the ground. In that age every dream was accounted a direct revelation from heaven. The interpretation of this one was not difficult. Only the poorest of the poor eat the despised barley. But these remorseless Bedouins had left to the despoiled inhabitants of Palestine nothing else. Their descendants still scornfully call the inoffensive inhabitants whom they plunder "barley-eaters." The awe-stricken listener makes at once the application. "This is nothing else," he says, "save the sword of Gideon." Israel's leader accepts the omen. He beckons to his armor-bearer. The two creep away as stealthily as they came. Gideon is impatient now for the conflict to begin, the issue of which is thus supernaturally assured to him.

He divides his little troop into three companies, the usual division of the Hebrew army. He gives to each a trumpet. He furnishes each with a peculiar torch, which burns with a dull, smouldering light, that blazes up in a sudden illumination when waved through the air. To conceal it more effectually, he orders the burning end to be covered with an earthen pot. This torch of Gideon is still carried as a dark lantern by the night-police of Cairo.

These preparations occupy probably the succeeding day. By sunset all is ready to inaugurate this most extraordinary campaign. In the silence and darkness of the night these three curiously-equipped companies steal across the valley of Jezreel. They environ the unsuspecting camp. By eleven o'clock they have taken their respective positions. Gideon gives the appointed signal. Almost at the same instant the earthen jars are broken and cast upon the ground; the torches, waving through the air, illume the hill-sides with a lurid light; the three hundred trumpets sound simultaneously the charge; the war-cry, "The sword of the Lord and of Gideon," echoes among the hills. The startled Midianites spring from their tents. The heterogeneous host is thrown into inextricable confusion. A panic ensues, like that which pervaded the Roman army when Hannibal, imitating the stratagem of Gideon, drove in upon their sleeping camp, among the defiles of the Apennines, the two thousand frightened oxen bearing lighted torches bound upon their horns. Trained to border warfare, these Bedouins are utterly unprepared to resist the surprise of such an unexpected assault. There is no Fabius, wise to reassure and to restrain them. Composed of different tribes and clans, speaking different tongues, under different leaders, banded together by no common nationality, only by a desire of booty or a wild passion of revenge, in the delirium of excitement they turn their swords upon each other.

For a brief hour a strange battle rages. Israel witnesses the slaughter of her foes without sharing in it. Then the Arabs flee through the darkness for the ford of Bethabara, their terrors intensified by their superstition, their dread of the unknown enemy the greater because he is undiscerned. Their road lays through the land of Ephraim. Its men of war, answering the call of Gideon's heralds, gather at the ford. The chief Midianitish kings have already passed over. Two of their subordinate sheiks are, however, captured. To such a foe, in such an hour of excitement, no mercy is shown. Their heads are brought as trophies to Gideon. He meanwhile, with his three hundred men, pursues the flying Arabs far into their own desert. Faint with two nights of watching and a long and rapid march, he yet rests not, till, surprising them again in their retreat, he has captured their chiefs, Zebah and Zalmunnah, and avenged the death of his own brethren by the execution of their murderers. So effectual is the rout, that, of one hundred and twenty thousand Bedouins, fifteen thousand alone survive. So thoroughly does Gideon follow it up, and such a lesson does he teach these untamable sons of the desert, that, for nearly half a century, Israel suffers no new incursion at their hands.

"Thus was Midian subdued before the children of Israel, so that they lifted up their heads no more; and the country was in quietness forty years in the days of Gideon."

The story of Gideon is a symbol as well as a history. God conducts all his campaigns upon analogous principles. The emancipation of mankind is always wrought out by a forlorn hope. God is *not* on the side of the strong battalions. In moral conflicts, at least, numbers never count. Only the few have faith in God and courage in his cause; and faith and courage alone gain the battle. Elijah faces alone the four hundred and fifty prophets of Baal. The schools of Hillel and Shammai are overturned by the unlearned Galilean fishermen. The religion of half of Europe is revolutionized by the ore-digger's son. The little Mayflower, tossed on the tempestuous seas of the Atlantic, suffices to bring across seed enough to plant half a continent with truth. A few men and women of the commoner classes gather for prayer and conference in Philip Embury's carpenter's shop. The aristocracy of New York disdain to associate with them. But the result of the prayers of these despised Methodists is the largest Protestant organization in America. Wilberforce in England, and William Lloyd Garrison in America, call for recruits to wage war against the combined interests, commercial, political, and ecclesiastical, of slavery and the slave-trade. Their adherents at first hardly equal in number Gideon's band; but they emancipate two continents.

Who would not chose to have been one of God's three hundred? But when he brings us to the Spring of Trembling, how rarely we covet the post of honor. How we shrink from the battle of the present, even while we honor the heroism that courted it in the past. Every era has its battle. God's trumpet calls to-day, as Gideon's did, for recruits. Enter the ranks. Get your commission and your equipments from God; then demand the surrender of your enemies and his in the spirit with which Ethan Allen demanded that of Ticonderoga: "In the name of the Great Jehovah and the Continental Congress."

Various attempts have been made to explain the principle upon which God selected Gideon's troop of three hundred. Josephus tells us that they were the cowards of the camp. Apparently he thinks thus to increase the wonder of the miracle. Stanley suggests directly the opposite explanation. "The next step was to remove the rash. At the brink of the spring, those who rushed headlong down to quench their thirst, throwing themselves on the ground, or plunging themselves into the water, were rejected; those who took up the water in their hands, and lapped it with self-restraint, were chosen." The Bible, however, does not suggest any interpretation of the singular test which God employed. He never acts without reason; but he very often refuses to give one. He chooses his own instruments for his work. He gives no account of the principle upon which he proceeds in their selection. The battle of life is not a guerrilla warfare. It is a divinely-ordered campaign. God selects his soldiers as he will. His tests of character are certainly widely different from our own, often quite incomprehensible to us. He makes sad havoc of our scholastic and theological measurings. A keen observer of life told me that he had watched for the future of twelve succeeding valedictorians of a certain New England college. Of only two did he ever hear any thing thereafter. One of those was a sailor. Mr. Moody, the famous lay preacher of Chicago, applied for admission to a New England Church when a young man, but was kept waiting for a year because he did not know enough of the doctrines. In less than a year after his admission, he had commenced, in his adopted city, a work for Christ, whose far-reaching influence is not surpassed by any pastor in the place. The God who passed by the seven manly sons of Jesse, and chose for royal honors the ruddy-faced boy brought in haste from the sheepfold, puzzles us as much as he did David's father by his singular method of selection. He sets aside America's trained statesmen, and commissions the rail-splitter to be her emancipator. He leaves Erasmus in his scholarship, and calls the singer-boy of Mansfield to liberate Europe. He selects not from the bishops, and deans, and canons of England's favored Church, but from her corps of unhonored and imperfectly-educated school ushers, the Spurgeon whose voice reaches most effectually the masses. What was once said by a famous divine of a celebrated revival preacher, may be said of nearly all the men whom God honors: "I do not doubt that God blesses his work, but I can not see why." He educates men, but his schooling is as singular as his selection. The most effectual temperance orator of England or America was picked from the gutter. The great reformer of the Church was educated a monk. The emancipator of America was born in a slave state. Paul sat at the feet of Gamaliel. Moses was brought up in Egypt.

There is but one principle of choice apparent in these cases, namely, that "God hath chosen the foolish things of the world to confound the wise; and God hath chosen the weak things of the world to confound the things which are mighty; and base things of the world, and things which are despised, hath God chosen, yea, and things which are not, to bring to nought things that are." Of this principle history contains many sublime illustrations; none so sublime as that which the Master himself affords. Does your cause seem feeble, your comrades few, your arms inadequate, the foe invincible, the campaign hopeless of success?

Consider him whose life so sublimely illustrates his own aphorism: The last shall be first, and the first last. The Crucified is become Conqueror. The very instrument of his death is become the symbol of religion. He that was without form or comeliness has reclothed a mourning world in beauty. The despised cake of barley has overturned the tents of Midian. The world itself is redeemed by the forlorn hope of Israel.

JEPHTHAH'S DAUGHTER.

## XI.
## THE PRICE OF AMBITION.

READERS of the Bible are apt to transfer the characteristics of the book and its sacred penmen to the people whose history it describes. They read in the Pentateuch the admirable code of laws which Moses, under the inspiration of God, framed for the government of Israel, and they are apt to take it for granted that those laws interpret the life and character of the people. The truth is, however, that the history of a nation is rarely, if ever, reflected in its legislation. It certainly was not in the case of Israel. The laws were divine. The history is intensely human. The laws were founded upon principles which humanity does not yet fully comprehend. The nation was in its infancy, a nation of just emancipated slaves, whose character is reproduced in the wild and lawless tribes which still inhabit the same country.

So long as Israel remained in the wilderness, the laws which God had given them were probably maintained in force with a good degree of perfection. The tabernacle traveled with them. The statutes could be read to the assembled people in frequent convocations. The priests and Levites were ready always to guard against infractions of a system upon the preservation of which their authority, their very existence as an order, depended. The people, gathered in a single camp, were easily governed, felt the influence of Moses's master-mind, and suffered but little temptation to adopt the rites, the laws, or the customs of heathen nations, with whom, indeed, they had little or nothing to do. During the first years of their occupation of the land of Canaan they were kept together by a common danger. Engaged in war, still possessing the character of a military encampment, still acting as one people under the guidance of Joshua, as they had before acted under the guidance of Moses, they doubtless preserved, measurably unimpaired, that religious and political system on which their national safety depended.

But if peace hath her victories no less than war, it is also true that she has her dangers. These Israel did not escape. The conquest was completed. The land was divided among the various tribes. The people settled down to cultivate the country which they had conquered. The leaders, whose personal influence had preserved the national unity, died. The law was no longer read to the people in yearly convocation. There were no copies of it scattered among the people, and no ability in them to read it if it had been. There were no local churches; nothing analogous to the synagogues which later, in every town and village, kept alive a remembrance of God's word. The Holy City was not yet founded. There was no central temple whither the people resorted. The nation no longer preserved its unity. The tribes, when not engaged in battling with surrounding nations, were engaged in quarrels among themselves. Infractions of the law were left unpunished. The law itself lapsed almost into oblivion. The Church lost its power. The priests and Levites themselves became corrupted by the forms of idolatry which almost universally prevailed. Alliances were formed with heathen nations; and such alliances brought into the Hebrew Church the heathen deities. As Rome subjugated Greece, but accepted her religion, and so intertwined it with her own that it is now quite impossible to separate Grecian and Roman mythology; as the Goths and Vandals in turn conquered Rome, but were themselves conquered by her half Christian, half heathen faith, so Israel conquered Canaan, but, as soon as the victory was complete, yielded her faith to that of the people she subdued. The consequence was a mongrel religion, in which the rites of heathenism and the worship of Jehovah were mingled in a most curious manner, and a lawless state of society in which "every man did that which was right in his own eyes." Thus, from the death of Joshua to the birth of Samuel, a space of about three hundred years, the people of Israel lived in a state of anarchy as much worse than that which characterized the first ten years of California's settlement as the era 1400 B.C. was more barbaric than that of 1800 A.D. This change in the condition of the Jewish nation is very simply indicated in the Bible in a single sentence: "The people served the Lord all the days of Joshua, and all the days of the elders that outlived Joshua, who had seen all the great works of the Lord that he did for Israel; * * * and there arose another generation after them which knew not the Lord, nor yet the works which he had done for Israel. And the children of Israel did evil in the sight of the Lord, and served Baalim."

The book of Judges describes in considerable detail this period of Jewish history. It affords a striking illustration of the truth, which statesmen and legislators are apt to forget, that the prosperity of a nation depends far less upon the nature of its laws than upon the condition and character of its people; that legislation is altogether secondary to education. Of the various graphic stories which it tells illustrative of the nature of this wild age, one of the most striking is that of Jephthah.

The tribe of Gad preserved, through all the changes of its Egyptian servitude and its pilgrimage in the wilderness, the characteristics which belonged to the patriarchs. It was a tribe of nomadic herdsmen, wild, warlike, rejoicing, as the Bedouin Arabs still do, in the freedom of the wilderness. They had selected for themselves a habitation in the district beyond the Jordan, a wild, weird region, which even now only the more daring and adventurous of Oriental tourists visit. In the highest state of civilization which Israel ever reached, the hills of Gilead were peopled by a wild and warlike race, who still continued, under the kings as under the judges, to do every man that which was right in his own eyes. There the sons of Saul maintained a shadow of their father's authority long after Judah had accepted David as their king. There, among the sons of Gad, David in turn selected some of his best captains, "men of might and men of war, fit for the battle, that could handle shield and buckler, whose faces were like the faces of lions, and were as swift as the roes upon the mountains." There, too, he found a retreat from his son Absalom. An exile from Judah, he was received with characteristic hospitality by this turbulent but chivalric people, who "brought beds, and basins, and earthen vessels, and wheat, and barley, and flour, and parched corn, and beans, and lentiles, and parched pulse, and honey, and butter, and sheep, and cheese of kine, for David and for the people that were with him, to eat." There he gathered up his army again; and, going forth from this wilderness, his captains fought the battle which ended in the death of his son Absalom, and the re-establishment of his authority.

Of this tribe Jephthah was a member. He was an illegitimate son. His brethren would have nothing to do with him, and drove him from the inheritance. He fled to the outskirts of the land, where Canaan bordered on the heathen wilderness. There he gathered about him a troop of wild and lawless men like himself, and became their acknowledged chieftain, leading the life of a freebooter, and often, doubtless, making just such incursions into the fields of Gilead as the Scottish clans used to make into the lowlands in the early history of Great Britain. Such a man soon acquires a certain sort of reputation, and Jephthah was known through all the trans-Jordanic region for a man of valor in an age when valor covered a multitude of sins. If the more peaceful inhabitants dreaded his forays, they doubtless told with pride the stories of his engagements with their nearest neighbors and worst foes, the Ammonites; for we may safely assume that, with the impartiality of brigandage, Jephthah was at least quite as ready to forage on their flocks as on those of his native tribe.

Thus it happened that, when war, always smouldering between the Hebrews and the heathen, broke out into an open flame between the tribe of Gad and the children of Ammon, the people instinctively looked to this Jephthah to become their leader, and a delegation of their sheiks went in person into the land of Tob to invite him to become their captain.

A man of the highest patriotic impulse would have led his wild companions straightway against the common foe. With Jephthah, personal self-seeking mingles with better motives. The opportunity to bargain for place is too good to be passed over. So he makes as though he were reluctant to accept the leadership, and demands, as his compensation, that, if he succeeds, he shall be made the chieftain of Israel. The terms are accepted. He is appointed. He sends an embassy to the Ammonites; demands the cause of their invasion; exhausts diplomacy before he resorts to arms; applies to his neighbors across the Jordan for an alliance; can get no aid from them, and makes ready for independent action. For meanwhile the Ammonites have penetrated into the heart of Gilead. There is no time for delay. Jephthah's tribe must fight single-handed the children of Ammon.

This is quite a different matter from any of the marauding expeditions which have hitherto constituted his sole military experience. The responsibility presses heavily on him. He is without advisers. He takes counsel of his superstitious fancies. He solemnly vows to offer as a burnt-offering to the Lord whatsoever comes forth to meet him from his house if he return in triumph. This is the price he is willing to pay for victory. He hardly stops, perhaps, to consider the full meaning of his promise. His campaign is a short but brilliant one. In a single battle the Ammonites are so utterly routed that they retreat without attempting to make a second stand. Twenty cities fall into his hands as the result of that decisive battle. The land of Gilead is effectually redeemed. Jephthah returns in triumph to the city of Mizpeh, which apparently serves as a sort of capital for the trans-Jordanic tribes.

Among those whose hearts beat high with exultation at this national deliverance there is none more joyous than Jephthah's daughter. She prepares to do her father honor; breaks over that maidenly reserve which forbids the Jewish maiden even to walk abroad unveiled and unattended, and, in the exuberance of her exultation, comes forth with timbrels and dances to meet him. So it is that the first one upon whom his eyes fall as he approaches his house in the city of Mizpeh is she who is the light of his home and the hope of his future. The sun that makes that hour bright is instantly beclouded. The joy of his victory gives place to the anguish of a riven heart. To the glad congratulations of his daughter, proud of her father's achievements and glad in her country's redemption, he cries out, "Alas! my daughter, thou hast brought me very low, and thou art one of them that trouble me; for I have opened my mouth unto the Lord, and I can not go back."

Over the dark scene which ensued Scripture drops a veil which we will not essay to draw aside. Of the bitter conflict between Jephthah's superstitious conscience and his heart's love; of the outcry of his distracted soul in the first strange revulsion of that hour; of the daughter's calm submission to the decree of death; of her solemn preparation in solitude among the mountains of Gilead; of the national grief in what is rightfully accounted a national affliction; and of the honor which a nation and an age that accounted woman of little worth paid for years thereafter to the memory of the self-consecrated maiden—of this we have but a faint suggestion in the brief and enigmatical narrative of Scripture: "And she said unto her father, 'Let this thing be done for me: let me alone two months, that I may go up and down upon the mountains and bewail my virginity, I and my fellows.' And he said, 'Go.' And he sent her away for two months; and she went with her companions, and bewailed her virginity upon the mountains. And it came to pass, at the end of two months, that she returned unto her father, who did with her according to his vow which he had vowed; and she knew no man. And it was a custom in Israel that the daughters of Israel went yearly to lament the daughter of Jephthah, the Gileadite, four days in a year."

We call this narrative enigmatical; for what is the true

interpretation of it is a question which has long divided Biblical critics, and which will probably never be satisfactorily settled. On the one hand, it is said that the language of the original text is ambiguous; that it is capable of a translation such as will only indicate that Jephthah consecrated whatever he should first meet to the Lord, but not necessarily as a burnt-offering; that the probability of his meeting a human being must have been in his mind when he uttered this vow, and that it is incredible that he should have promised to offer such an offering upon God's altar; that, even if he had made such a vow, the high-priest would have assuredly interfered to prevent the consummation of a sacrifice in direct violation of the religion of Israel; that the people themselves, who were so horrified at a similar sacrifice when offered by the King of Moab, and interfered to prevent Saul from putting to death his own son under circumstances which offered greater palliation, would never have suffered Jephthah to fulfill his cruel purpose; that the law made special provision for the redemption by money of any subject consecrated to sacrifice—a law of which Jephthah would have been sure to avail himself; that, if the execution had really taken place, the Bible would have described it in language more explicit, would have condemned it in language not unambiguous, and would certainly not have included Jephthah among the heroes whose faith is commended, as it is in the eleventh chapter of Hebrews, for our imitation; and that, finally, the direct declaration of the history that her companions "bewailed her virginity," and that "she knew no man," indicate a consecration to a life of seclusion as a virgin—a self-sacrifice far more significant among the Hebrews, in that age, than it is in Christendom at the present day. These considerations are very strongly seconded by those commendable sympathies which make us naturally reluctant to conceive it possible that any thing so unnatural and horrible as the literal sacrifice of a daughter by her father could take place, under the impulse of mistaken religious motives, especially in the supposed service of the true God, and at the hands of one who honestly sought to serve and please him.

On the other hand, it is said that the plain language of the narrative is that Jephthah vowed to consecrate as a burnt-offering whatever came forth to meet him; that so the narrative was read by all Hebrew scholars, Jewish and Christian, until as late as the twelfth century; that to change the translation to meet preconceived views is always a false philology and a dangerous exegesis; that vows of celibacy were absolutely unknown and unheard of, not only among the Hebrews, but among surrounding nations; that to attribute such a vow to Jephthah is to impute to an era fourteen centuries before Christ the religious ideas and customs of the mediæval ages of Christianity; that, on the other hand, human sacrifices were of very common occurrence in the Orient among all people except the Hebrews; that Abraham himself supposed at one time that he was called upon by God to offer up a similar sacrifice; that it is not strange that the more humane principles of the Mosaic religion and legislation were not yet fully comprehended by the semi-barbarous Gileadites, or by Jephthah, whose life had been spent probably as much among the heathen as among the people of God; that it was not a more marked violation of the law than was the act of Gideon in setting up an unauthorized, if not an idolatrous worship in Ophrah; that at the time of this occurrence there was as yet no order of prophets established to keep alive a popular remembrance of the law and obedience to its precepts; that the Levites themselves were as much corrupted by idolatrous associations as the people; that the high-priest was in the adjoining but hostile tribe of Ephraim, unable alike to participate in the sacrifice, as he is represented by legendary art to have done, or to protest against it; that the very vagueness of the narrative indicates a horror so fearful that the pen recoiled from its narration; that the principle of the sacred penmen is to narrate, not to approve or condemn, and that therefore it passes by in silence this fearful sacrifice, leaving the story itself to make its own impression—an impression which words of condemnation could only weaken; that if the name of Jephthah is included among those the record of whose faith the apostle thinks worthy of our imitation, so also are the names of Rahab, who was a harlot, and of David, who was guilty of the double crime of murder and adultery, and that the whole teaching of that remarkable chapter is lost by those who fail to perceive that it is *faith*, not purity, the power of which the apostle alone seeks to illustrate—faith often mated to ignorance or marred by sin; and that, finally, the Scripture, in saying of the daughter of Jephthah that "she knew no man," simply points out the fact, which gives significance to the whole of this strange story, that Jephthah was left by his singular vow without issue, and that therefore the hope of founding a dynasty, which had lured him from his retreat in the land of Tob, was destroyed at the same moment that his own power and position was rendered secure by his victory.

Whichever of these views is entertained, the fact remains that Jephthah sacrificed his daughter to his political ambition. Whether he did so by a literal or an emblematic offering, it is neither important, nor, perhaps, possible to determine with certainty. The moral of his history is the same. Jephthah realized his dream. He judged Israel to the day of his death. But at what a cost! It was better far to be an outlaw in the land of Tob with his daughter's companionship, than to be ruler in the land of Gilead with the gloom of her sacrifice shadowing his heart. Was there ever a time thereafter that, in the wretched loneliness of his rude court at Mizpeh, he did not look back with regret on his tent life in the wilderness?

We wonder that Jephthah should have made a vow so vague, the consequences of which might prove so terrible. But Jephthah's vow is not an unusual one. It is repeated, half consciously, yet with a terrible earnestness, by every man who, setting out in life, resolves to attain his victory —wealth, honor, power—cost what it may. This terrible history is re-enacted by every one who pays, as the price of his ambition, the light and joy of his true life. We shudder at the sacrifice of a daughter as though it were an event of rare occurrence. Is it indeed so? When I read of courtly marriages between princes and potentates, where crowns, not hearts, are joined, and, to extend or maintain a kingdom, a noble nature, possessing wondrous capabilities of love, is sacrificed to political expediency, I think of Jephthah and his daughter. When I see society gathering to crown with mocking festivities the immolation of a fair maiden in a cruel, loveless marriage, the price of social ambition, I think of Jephthah and his daughter. When I see the man of business so immersed in the toils of life that his children grow up neglected—for it is the children of the rich, not of the poor, that suffer most from neglect —provided by their father with all that money can purchase, and with nothing else, his daughters priestesses in the court of fashion, his sons sowing in idleness and dissipation the seeds of future debauchery and drunkenness, I think of Jephthah and his daughter. Only Jephthah sacrificed to Jehovah under the impulse of a misguided conscience, we to Mammon under the dictation of sordid hopes. He sacrificed a daughter, we every thing that makes life worth living. The tradesman who sacrifices honesty to profits, the lawyer who sacrifices justice to victory, the politician who sacrifices patriotism to place, the minister who sacrifices God's truth to pulpit popularity—what are they but modern Jephthahs, guilty of a greater folly and a greater sin. A noble ambition, rightly directed, is essential to a true life—a truth we shall presently see illustrated by the story of Samson. But ambition crowned monarch becomes a most tyrannical and despoiling despot, that taxes heavily and gives little in return, a very Abimelech among kings, a very bramble of a monarch, out of which comes fire that devours the cedars of Lebanon.

It is better to live an outlaw in the land of Tob than to sacrifice one's true life for any post, however alluring, in the land of Gilead. This, as we read it, is the moral of the story of Jephthah and his daughter.

SAMSON AND DELILAH.

## XII.

## SAMSON'S STRENGTH AND WEAKNESS.

FROM the wild and rocky fastnesses of the trans-Jordanic region, history conducts us to the fertile plains which border the Mediterranean Sea.

Of these plains, which constitute one of the great physical features of the Holy Land, the richest and most fertile was that of Philistia. Its sea-port towns rendered it capable of a maritime commerce in an age of the world when the Mediterranean bordered civilization, and was universally known as the Great Sea. Its territory, lying midway between Egypt, mother of civilization, and Phœnicia, mother of language, rendered it a great highway. Its fertile soil, watered by the streams which flow from the adjoining hills of Judea, was always fruitful, abounding with the wheat, the olive, and the grape, even in times when famine cursed adjoining lands. Its level plains afforded facilities for horses and chariots of war which the hill-country of Palestine did not possess, and thus contributed to render its people peculiarly warlike. Never really subdued by Joshua, the Philistines continued to maintain a desultory guerrilla warfare against the neighboring tribes, until finally subjugated in the long campaigns which David waged against them. At the time of which we write, however, they were really masters of nearly all the country west of the Jordan valley. They carried their incursions as far north as Jezreel, as far east as the Jordan. The Israelites, divided by petty jealousies, not infrequently engaged in civil war among themselves, proved no match for their powerful neighbors. Their resistance to these inroads became less and less vigorous, and finally altogether ceased. The tribes of Israel became tributaries to the land of Philistia. They lost all heart; had no courage to respond to the call of Samson; with their own hands bound their would-be deliverer, and surrendered him to their oppressors. National degradation can go no farther.

Such was the condition of the western tribes when Samson was born. He was of the tribe of Dan, of the town of Zorah. His birth was heralded by an angelic messenger. In accordance with the divine command, he was consecrated to the life of a Nazarite, from his cradle, by his mother's vows. He drank no wine; ate no grapes; suffered the locks of his hair to grow uncut. From his youth he gave tokens of that extraordinary strength which has since rendered his name proverbial. His fame was not confined to his own nation. Under the title of Hercules he was deified both in Egypt and in Greece; for that Hercules is a heathen transformation of Samson there is little room to doubt. To the same symbolic origin both names are traced by linguists. Both are men of superhuman strength, of exuberant physical life, of wild, ungovernable passions, and of broad and trenchant humor. Of both substantially the same traditions are told. Both slay a lion with their own hands. Both suffer death, though in different ways, at the hands of their treacherous wives. One, a captive in Philistia, summoned to make sport for his enemies, pulls down the temple of Dagon, and buries both the god and its worshipers in the ruins. The other, a captive in Egypt, is led forth to be sacrificed to Jupiter, breaks the bands which bind him, and slays the priests and scatters the assemblage. Even the custom of tying a lighted torch between two foxes in the circus, in the memory of the damage once done to the harvest by a fox with burning hay and straw tied to it, was long maintained in Greece, a singular witness to the extent of Samson's reputation.

Yet, with all his power and prowess, Samson's life proves a most wretched failure. "He justifies no expectation, lives to no purpose, and goes out finally, as a snuffed candle, at the end of a most foolish and absurd life."

We first meet him on his way to Timnath. A Philistine maiden has captured his fancy by her beauty. His parents remonstrate against the alliance. "Is there never a woman among the daughters of thy brethren, or among all my people, that thou goest to take a wife of the uncircumcised Philistines?" But neither the protests of his parents, nor the plain provisions of the law, nor the high and holy mission to which he is called by God, can counteract his passion. To Timnath he will go.

The result justifies the father's remonstrance. The Philistine maiden plays the coquette with Samson. He proposes, as is the custom in the Orient, a riddle to his guests at the betrothal feast. He wagers with them thirty changes of raiment that they can not guess it. She cajoles him out of his secret, and discloses it. That they should have won the wager does not trouble him. He goes alone, across the country, and takes the thirty changes of raiment from the Philistine city of Ashkelon to pay his bet. But that he should have been cheated by a woman sorely wounds his pride; and when the Philistine coquette marries one of these very guests, Samson's groomsman, his indignation knows no bounds. This is the beginning of hostilities. Samson, to avenge himself of his enemy, catches three hundred jackals, ties them together two by two by the tails, puts a firebrand between the tails, and sets them loose in the harvest season to set fire to the Philistines' standing wheat. Then, when the Philistines, with a singular injustice, visit their wrath on the bride and the father, putting her to death, Samson, with that fickleness of feeling which characterizes him, smites them "hip and thigh with a great slaughter."

We next find him in the hands of more formidable foes. The Philistines come up to avenge their wrongs on the nation which shelters him. The Israelites deliver him bound into their hands. He submits without opposition, only to break the cords that bind him, and leap upon his would-be captors with a shout that fills them with alarm. In the panic which ensues a thousand are slain—some, doubtless, by Samson's own hand, others perhaps trampled under foot by their own companions.

Twenty years elapse, during which he is acknowledged as the leader of his own tribe, and perhaps also of the neighboring tribes of Judah and Benjamin. Doubtless the authority of the Philistines is broken, their yoke somewhat lightened; doubtless, too, his term of office is marked by constant raids and border warfare. It is not, however, characterized by any marvelous achievements on Samson's part, whom nothing seems capable of arousing but personal wrongs or imminent danger. We next meet him, at all events, in Gaza, a Philistine city, whither he has gone in pursuit of a Philistine harlot, still yielding to the bane of his life, an unbridled, self-willed, self-indulgent spirit. The Philistines close the gates, and set a watch to catch him at the dawn. At midnight he goes out, takes the gates and their posts, and carries them off, in a sort of scornful disdain of their boasted strength, and so escapes.

One might have thought he would have learned enough by this time of Philistine women. But such a man, weak in the very self-conceit of his own strength, never learns. He falls in with another, sets his heart upon her, and, with a folly for which there is absolutely no palliation, walks with open eyes into the trap this treacherous Delilah sets for him. She undertakes to get from him the secret of his superhuman strength. Three times he mocks her with lying answers. Three times she binds him, and delivers him into the Philistines' hands. He breaks the green withes, the new ropes, the web woven in with his hair, and scatters the captors, who imagine that they have secured him. Three times he discovers the treachery of this woman; and yet, because of her beauty, and yielding to her tears and entreaties, he deliberately tells her the whole secret of his strength, then lies down to sleep with his head upon her lap, to awaken, his locks shaven, his vow broken, his strength gone, and himself an easy prey to his remorseless enemies.

If his life had ended here there would have been nothing in it to entitle him to a place among the heroes of Hebrew history; nothing to explain the fact that the apostle names him among those who "through faith subdued kingdoms." But his servitude teaches him that lesson of self-denial which nothing but affliction suffices to teach. He grinds away in the prison-house of his foes; employs, in this horrid slavery, the remnant of that strength with which God had endowed him, and which, by her vows, his mother had consecrated to God's service. Little by little that strength returns to him. At last he is brought forth on one of the high days of the Philistines to grace a heathen festival. Humbled, he looks to God for strength to fulfill his purpose, and redeems his name from the ignominy which would otherwise attach to his wasted life by voluntarily sacrificing himself that he may win one more victory over the Philistines, and bury their god Dagon in its own temple.

"And Samson said, Let me die with the Philistines. And he bowed himself with all his might; and the house fell upon the lords, and upon all the people that were therein; so the dead which he slew at his death were more than they which he slew in his life. Then his brethren, and all the house of his father, came down and brought him up, and buried him between Zorah and Eshtaol, in the burying-place of Manoah his father."

If you will consider it, this story of Samson is not more remarkable for its narration of his marvelous physical strength than for its display of his marvelous moral weakness—"his impotence of mind in body strong." In this age of much-praised muscular Christianity, it is worth our while to notice of how little use the muscular is without the Christianity; to repeat to ourselves Samson's self-questioning in his captivity, as Milton portrays it:

> "What is strength without a double share
> Of wisdom? Vast, unwieldy, burthensome,
> Proudly secure, yet liable to fall
> By weakest subtleties; not made to rule,
> But to subserve where wisdom bears command."

Samson's virtues and vices are those of one in whom the animal nature predominates. He is bold, fearless, audacious; rushes into all sorts of hazards with the recklessness of an untamable self-reliance; engages with the lion for the mere sport of rare wrestling; goes alone across the country of the Philistines to forage in the city of Ashkelon for the means of paying his wager; goes down to the walled city of Gaza, when he well knows that all Philistia is on the watch for him; puts himself into Delilah's hands over and over again when he has already discovered her treachery. With this rare strength and aimless courage goes the good humor which belongs to exuberant health and vigor. His very name, "The Sunny," indicates this quality, which manifests itself oftenest in his deeds, yet sometimes in his speech, as in his reply to the discoverers of his secret: "If ye had not plowed with my heifer ye had not found out my riddle." "His most valiant, his most cruel actions are done with a smile on his face and a jest in his mouth." "He is full of the spirits and the pranks, no less than of the strength of a giant." His half-humorous revenge on the Philistines for the treachery of the coquette who jilted him; his assault on his foes with the ridiculous weapon, the jaw-bone of an ass; his scornful song of triumph over them; his huge jest on the inhabitants of Gaza in carrying off their gates; his trick, thrice repeated, on Delilah—all characterize a man of buoyant temper and effervescing life, too full of animal spirits to take aught seriously, to feel in any measure the bitterness of his nation's servitude, or to give himself to its deliverance.

So this very strength of his animal nature proves his weakness and works his ruin. Inspired by no high, noble, commanding purpose, his misdirected power spends itself in fitful gusts of idle bravado; he fails to fulfill the mission with which God has intrusted him, and, instead of setting his people free, suffers the chains to be welded on his own wrists. Endowed with superhuman strength, he is yet unable to control his own untamable passions. He is wholly wanting in the power of self-restraint. So, like a rudderless ship, blown hither and thither by the impulses of the hour, the very strength of his own nature only makes his wreck and ruin the more terrible. Upon his monument might fittingly be inscribed, "Died, by his own hand, a victim of self-indulgence." To the protest of his parents against his marriage with a Philistine maiden, the answer is, to him, all-sufficient, "It is right in *mine* eyes." He inaugurates a campaign against the oppressors of his people, not in any well-considered purpose to deliver them, but in a mere half-humorous, half-savage freak of personal revenge. He breaks the bonds with which Israel had bound him. A man of true moral courage would never have been bound; would have awakened in the hearts of his people a courage like his own, and led them to a victory which would not have been fruitless. It is true, he delivers himself from the town of Gaza by a marvelous feat of strength; but the weakness which could suffer him, a judge in Israel, to pursue a Philistine harlot into the trap there set for him was yet more marvelous. He slays a thousand Philistine men of arms, but he is unable to resist the tears and blandishments of one Philistine woman; breaks the new ropes as though they were threads of tow, but is curiously powerless to break the web she weaves about him. Ordained of God from his cradle to be a deliverer of his people, the ambition to deliver them never seems to have actuated him. He lives an aimless, and therefore a barren life. He dies a fruitless, though a martyr's death. His nation remains in the bondage from which he might have freed it, and his name survives him only to witness to the weakness of him whose powers, however great they may be, are subservient to his passions. Jephthah sacrificed his heart's affections to his ambition. We lament his folly while we honor his fidelity. Samson sacrificed a high and holy ambition to the gratification of unbridled lust. Nothing but the pathos of his death saves his name from deserved oblivion.

In different forms the history of Samson is re-enacted on every side of us. It is not merely that young America is shorn of his strength, lying in the lap of indulgence. It is not merely that many a young giant, called of God to a noble mission, and gloriously endowed with all the power which talent, education, wealth, friends, position give, casts all recklessly away for the sake of an hour of self-gratification with the treacherous Delilah. It is not merely that his worst foes hide their wiles beneath the witchery and enticements of pleasure, which ancient mythology rightly pictured as a beautiful but treacherous woman. It is not merely that self-indulgence undermines the character, destroys the manhood, eats out the strength, and leaves the emasculated victim to fall an easy prey to the most degrading forms of servitude. All this, indeed, is true. No young man ever doubts the truth of this, or will deny the reality of the dangers which environ a life surrendered to illicit pleasure. But every young man expects to escape those dangers. Every Samson, when he enters Gaza, does so in full assurance that its walls can not imprison him. If he lies down in the lap of Delilah, it is in the confidence that he will arise as strong as ever. Did you ever know the young man who doubted his power to lay aside the cigar, drop the wine-cup, break off with corrupt companions, step aside from the path of illicit pleasure at his will? Does any man ever believe that he can be shorn of his strength? "Seest thou a man wise in his own conceit? There is more hope of a fool than of him."

But in the story of Samson's life is more than this. In its disclosure of his weakness it discloses the secret of all strength—a single purpose resolutely pursued. This can achieve any thing. First of all warriors, in ancient or modern times, is the Little Corporal, whose diminutive stature is the subject, at the outset of his career, of much coarse satire. First of all orators, in past or present ages, is the Greek youth whose thick utterance seemed to forbid all hope of eloquence. But, on the other hand, he who lacks a noble purpose lacks the first condition of true power. All the culture which a college curriculum affords is thrown utterly away by a large proportion of its students for want of a centralizing, crystallizing aim. An army without a commander is a mere mob. A man without a purpose is not a man. He is a mere *canaille* of disorganized appetites and passions. His forces may be never so great; if there is no master-passion to martial and direct all the rest, there will be no heroic battle, no victory. The moral of that threadbare fable of the tortoise and the hare is not that assiduity is better than genius, but that a persistent purpose is always fleeter than a fitful one. Some one has epitomized the condition of a true life in the sentence, "Have something to do, then do it." This first condition is how often disregarded. How many an antitype has Samson, whose life comes to nothing, not for want of capacity, nor yet for lack of opportunity, but for very aimlessness. Power misapplied—of how many lives this single sentence would be the all-sufficient history. How many a young man of noble nature, and almost divine endowment, called of God to live in an era when "to be living is sublime," yet casts his life utterly away, like early rotted fruit, for want of a sublime purpose, and a persistent pursuit of it. How many lives, as sadly gone to ruin as that of Samson, attest the truth of the wise man's apothegm, "He that hath no rule over his own spirit is like a city that is broken down and without walls."

## XIII.

### ELISHA'S VISION.

NEARLY three hundred years elapsed between the days of Samson and those of Elisha. Israel in the mean time underwent great changes. The republic was supplanted by the monarchy. Saul consolidated the tribes under one national government. David prepared the way, by his service of song, for the erection of the Temple and the establishment of its sublime ritualistic service. Solomon extended his domain beyond that of any predecessor. With peace and prosperity came luxury, sensuality, enervation. Both the vices and the virtues of his reign were significant of degradation. When immorality is rife, religion becomes a mere system of ethics. It was so in the days of Solomon. The religious teachings of his age ceased to appeal to the higher religious sentiments—appealed only to the moral sense. Religious experience deteriorated from a spiritual apprehension of the unseen to a half-sensual, emotional fervor. The book of Proverbs and Solomon's Song followed the inculcations of Samuel and Nathan, and the Psalms of David. The book of Proverbs is a collection of moral maxims. It inculcates chiefly the common virtues—chastity, honesty, industry, truth. It draws its sanctions chiefly from the rewards and punish-

M

ments of the present. It rarely refers to God or the future. Such a work is itself a sign of deteriorating morals, which its feeble protests are, however, quite powerless to correct. Solomon's Song is a book of religious experience. It is so steeped in the enervation of the age which begets it, that, to the present day, Biblical critics are not agreed whether it is a religious poem or an Oriental love-song. With the death of Solomon the glory of Judaism faded, never to revive. The kingdom was rent in twain. Ten tribes, occupying the northern portion of the common territory, took for their capital Shechem, the chief city of Samaria. The two tribes of Judah and Benjamin alone remained faithful to the dynasty of David.

From this time the corruption of Israel increased with fearful rapidity. The laws of God were openly, and by public proclamation, annulled. Idols were put up in Bethel and Dan, and the worship of the Egyptian calf was substituted for that of Jehovah. Under Ahab the worship of Baal became the national religion, the priests of Baal the ministers of the national Church. The disciples of Jehovah professed their religious faith at the hazard of life itself. The law of Moses providing for free speech became a dead letter. The prophets of God were not safe from the impious hands of the audacious king and his yet more audacious wife. Elijah fled from the court to the wilderness for safety. One hundred and fifty prophets took refuge in a cave from the persecutions of Jezebel. So thorough was the apparent extermination of God's people that Elijah supposed that he alone was left to worship the true God. The courts of justice imbibed the spirit of the age. The judges, creatures of the king, did the royal bidding, and covered with the forms of law acts of the most flagrant injustice.

This corruption proceeded at length to such a pass as to produce an inevitable reaction. If there had not been among the people a deep, strong, though unuttered sense of the nation's degradation, the priests of Baal never would have obeyed the summons of Elijah to the trial of their faith at Mount Carmel. The four hundred and fifty priests of the Phœnician god were slain by a popular uprising. The power of the court was broken. Jezebel was never able to restore it. Ahab was slain in battle. Ahaziah died, by an accident, after a short reign of two years. Jehoram, a younger brother, reigned in his stead. The queen, growing old, never acquired over him the influence she possessed over his father or his brother. The image of Baal was put away. The golden calves remained at Bethel and at Dan, and, although their worship constituted the religion of the state, apparently some measure of religious liberty was accorded to the people. Elisha was invited to the court which threatened his predecessor's life. He became one of the king's privy counselors. The campaign against the Moabites was conducted according to his advice, and their incursion was repelled, and they routed and driven from the land with great slaughter. This enhanced his reputation. He lived in state at the capital. His fame extended beyond the bounds of his own nation. Mild, gentle, not lacking in quiet courage, yet shrinking from public conflicts, he uttered no protest against the corruption of his age, though he never shared it, and endeavored to neutralize its pernicious tendencies rather by the quiet influence of his own simple habits and the example of his own godly life than by denunciations of irreligion and vice. He was the Melancthon, as Elijah was the Luther of his age.

Such was the condition of Israel at the time of which we write. Their land was overrun with marauding bands from Syria, as in the days of Gideon and Samson it had been overrun with similar companies from the land of Moab. The inhabitants had suffered not a little from these incursions. At length the King of Syria formed the design of taking captive the King of Israel himself. He prepared for this purpose, at different times, several ambuscades. But, however secretly his plans were formed, and however well and wisely executed, they came to naught. They were always discovered; the ambuscade was always avoided. The king was convinced that there was treachery in his camp. He held a council of war, and disclosed his suspicions to his chief officers. One of them undertook to defend himself and his companions from the imputation: "Elisha, the prophet that is in Israel," said he, "telleth the King of Israel the words that thou speakest in thy bedchamber." The surmise was not an unnatural one; for it is to be remembered that Naaman, captain of the host of Syria, and a great man with his master, had tested in his own person the power of this prophet. It is no wonder, therefore, that Elisha's reputation in the heathen court was second only to that which he enjoyed in the court of Israel. The theory of this officer, perhaps Naaman himself, was the correct one. It was accepted by the king, who resolved to capture the prophet, and so put an end to this disclosure of his plans. For this purpose he organized a much larger company than ordinary. He learned by spies that Elisha was at Dothan, a city whose ruins still remain to mark its site in the north of Samaria, not far from the plains of Esdraelon. He acted with such secrecy and such celerity that his designs were not suspected until the city was entirely surrounded, and escape seemed to be impossible.

Elisha's servant was the first to discover the Syrian encampment. He seems to have gone out in the early morning, perhaps for water, which in Palestine is usually drawn from wells without the city walls. He hurried back to his master in great consternation. "Alas! my master," he cried, "how shall we do?"

Elisha, however, manifested no discomposure. He replied in language which the Christian world has since adopted as its own: "Fear not; for they that be with us are more than they that be with them." The young man could not understand this language. He could see the chariots, and horses, and tents of Syria. He could see nothing able to withstand them. He had no conception of the declaration of David, "The angel of the Lord encampeth around about them that fear him, and delivereth them."

Elisha had compassion on his servant. Unable to inspire him with faith in an unseen God, the prophet besought the Lord to vouchsafe to this terrified rationalist a glimpse of the invisible guardians whose presence he seemed otherwise unable to comprehend. The request was granted. "And the Lord opened the eyes of the young man, and he saw; and behold, the mountain was full of horses and chariots of fire round about Elisha."

This sight seems to have been afforded solely to reassure the trembling heart of the servant. No use was made of the horses and chariots. The Syrians were smitten with a mental blindness, which made them fall easily into the snare which Elisha prepared for them. He went boldly out of the city to the Syrian camp. He made as if he would open negotiations with them. They told him they were not after prey, but after Elisha the prophet. "Follow me," said he, "and I will bring you to the man whom ye seek." He fulfilled his promise. But he did not disclose himself till he had brought them into the very heart of Samaria, where, surrounded by the armies of Israel, they were entirely at the mercy of Jehoram. The King of Israel was anxious to fall upon them and punish their temerity with the sword. But Elisha forbade, with some indignation: "Wouldest thou smite those whom thou hast taken captive with thy sword and with thy bow?" said he. Instead, he ordered a feast to be prepared for them. After they had partaken of it they were dismissed. Doubtless the King of Syria was equally surprised at the issue of his campaign, and at the unheard-of treatment which the captive army received. He seems to have been shamed for the time into peace; for the sacred historian closes his narration by telling us that "the bands of Syria came no more into the land of Israel."

In a religious point of view, the history of the world prior to the appearance of Christ may be briefly described as a struggle between the sensuous and the super-sensuous. That struggle was not confined to the Jewish people, nor were the educative influences, which gradually prepared the way for the life of faith on the earth, limited to Palestine. In India, Buddha protested, though in vain, against the gross idolatries of Brahminism. In China, Confucius made a similar, though no more successful attempt to supplant, with a cold but pure morality, the same imaginative but degrading worship. In Greece and Rome there were not a few pure spirits who dimly discerned and mystically interpreted the life of God in the soul. Yet, while the world has never been without some such witnesses, even in its darkest hours, on the whole the strong tendency of the human race has been to ignore the unseen world altogether. Probably to the vast majority of Christendom, and even to many Christians, Paul's expression, "We look not at the things which are seen, but at the things which are not seen," is a mystical expression, which they attribute to a poetical frame of mind, and interpret accordingly.

It is in an especial degree the tendency of the present age to deal only with tangible truths. Reason is the high-priest of the Nineteenth Century. It knows only the phenomena which the senses report to it. Its philosophy scouts the aphorism of Pascal, "The heart has reasons of its own that the reason knows not of." It tries every teaching by scientific tests; weighs moral truths in the apothecary's scales; sends divine and unseen realities to the chemists to be analyzed and tested.

But there is, nevertheless, an invisible world, which they only see whose eyes the Lord has opened. Science tells us a great deal; but there is a sphere which it is absolutely incompetent to enter; about which, question it as you may, it is absolutely dumb. It can analyze the flower, and tell you all its parts, and describe its wonderful mechanisms and their yet more wonderful operations; but it has neither the eye to discern nor the heart to feel the subtle influence of its divine beauty. It dissects with its keen scalpel the human frame, and tells you the nature and function of every part—what the heart supplies, what the nerves do, how the muscles act. But there is no anatomy possible of the soul; no microscope discloses the nature and the office of reason, imagination, love. The inner life hides itself from the baffled scientist. It needs the prophetic eye to discern the true man within. There are truths which can not be deduced; which are not wrought out with much thought and from much observation; which are incapable of logical demonstration. They are to be known, to be instantly apprehended by the soul upon the mere presentation of them. The musician can not prove that the harmonies of Mendelssohn or Beethoven are grand to one whose soul is not thrilled by them. The practical mill-man, who saw in Niagara nothing but a great water-power, was simply incapable of appreciating that "grandeur of the Creator's power" which led Audubon to bow before it trembling in silent adoration. Love can not be proved to a mother. The babe on her breast is the only demonstration. Disbelief in love is the evidence of an indurated heart. The man who misanthropically scouts at affection, only witnesses, by his skepticism, his own moral degradation.

It is of this unseen world the Bible treats. In the Old Testament times God revealed it to the race, still in childhood, by disclosures to the senses. Under the New Testament dispensation God reveals it to the race, advanced toward manhood, by developing within the soul a power of spiritual discernment. Rationalism expects us to prove all that we believe. There are beliefs that are far above all proof. Of them we can only say, "We speak that we do know, and testify that we have seen." Theology does not—at least it never ought to—rest on argument, but on experience. We believe not what is proved to us, but what we have felt in our own souls. Of such truths we say what Sam Johnson said of Free-will, "We know it, and that's the end on't."

Herbert Spencer has labored to demonstrate that it is impossible for the human soul to form any conception of God. Job's friend proved the same truism centuries before. Neither can the babe form any conception of its mother. It *knows* its mother nevertheless, cries when away from her, sleeps contented in her arms. Carlyle has said many foolish things and some wise ones, but none, I think, truer than this: "Of final causes, man, by the nature of the case, can *prove* nothing; knows them (if he know any thing of them), not by the glimmering flint-sparks of logic, but by an infinitely higher light of intuition." Atheism, by whatever *alias* it conceals itself, is simply blindness. Our faith in God rests not on arguments which prove his existence, but on the fact that we have felt his arms encircle us.

Doubtless Moses believed in God while he still remained in Egypt. He was familiar with those arguments by which the wise men, even of that polytheistic land, proved the existence of a Great First Cause. He had learned, through his mother's sacred instructions, of the God of his fathers. But after he had stood by the burning bush—after, in the solemn mountain-top, he had talked with Jehovah, did he need any longer to sustain his faith by these poor considerations? He who, on the more sacred Mount of Calvary, has seen his Savior through the gathering gloom, and talked there with his God as friend talketh with friend, needs no argument to prove to him that God *is*. Nor can all the cold logic of a Herbert Spencer countervail the witness of this experience. No man can by searching find out God. Science can never disclose him. Nevertheless, "Blessed are the pure in heart, for they shall *see* God." Science is supreme in her own dominion, but the unseen world is not within it.

All the arguments which philosophical theology brings to witness to the divinity and the atoning sacrifice of Christ, however useful as buttresses, are but poor foundation-stones for Christian faith in him. The four Gospels are the best Evidences of Christianity. Christ is his own highest witness. We accept him, not for his credentials, but for himself; not because he is proved to us to be the Son of God, but upon the mere sight of him. Worship is refused him only by those to whom he is not really known. Their eyes are holden that they can not see. I am sure that if any man saw the Jesus that I see, he would fall down before him crying "My Lord and my God." There are many who, like the young man, look up and see only clouds in the horizon. By-and-by the hand of Christ touches their eyes; the prayer of Christ intercedes for them, and with open eyes they behold, in what was before only the Son of the carpenter, the very Son of God. Not all the apostles could by their arguments have convinced the iron-hearted centurion. But when he saw that Jesus so cried out and gave up the ghost, he said, "Truly this man was the Son of God."

In short, there is a spiritual sense which directly and immediately perceives the world of invisible truth. In this domain it rules supreme. It has no rival, no peer. It alone is competent to investigate spiritual truth. The time will come when education will systematically develop this faculty, which it now systematically neglects; for at present it is unrecognized. Science has not heard of it. It finds no place in the customary classification of the faculties. Neither Hamilton, nor Spurzheim, nor Bain, nor Spencer recognize it. But the Bible is full of it. Life, in which are many things undreamed of in our yet partial philosophy, abounds in the manifestations of it. Moses witnesses to it. David sings of it. Isaiah, with more than mortal eloquence, portrays the immortal truths which it has revealed to him. Paul is endowed with preternatural power, because it discloses to him the sublime mysteries of the wisdom of God, which none of the princes of this world knew. And an innumerable host of Christians, strengthened, sustained, comforted by its hidden life, bear witness by their lives to its reality and its efficacy.

If, then, fellow-Christian, you are sometimes perplexed by arguments which you can not answer, recur to this hidden witness on whose testimony your faith is really founded. If the Bible is really the bread of life to your soul, if it gives comfort to you in affliction, peace in storm, victory in sore battle, you need no other evidence that it is the Word of God. If Christ is to you a present help, if you hear his voice counseling you, and see his luminous form guiding you, and hear in your own soul his message to your troubled conscience, "Peace, be still," you need no other argument, as you can have no higher one, that he is Savior and God to you. This sight of the soul is above all reason. Mary, hearing the message of the disciples that Christ was arisen, believed it not. Coming to the sepulchre, and finding it empty, even the declaration of the angel was insufficient to assure her. But the voice of her Lord, though he but uttered in well-known accents her name, "Mary," was enough. She doubted, could doubt no more. It is not on the witness of men, nor even on that of angels, our faith in a crucified and a risen Savior rests; but on this, that he has spoken our name, and turned, by the very sweetness of his voice, our night of weeping into a day of unutterable joy. "Now we believe, not because of thy saying; for we have heard him ourselves, and know that this is indeed the Christ, the Savior of the world."

If, on the other hand, reader, your soul is haunted by many doubts which the incantations of philosophy can not lay; if the cold creed of a Church stands between you and Christ; if love is waiting on knowledge, and you are delaying to follow Jesus until, by the slow processes of a blind and stumbling logic, you can analyze the scientific deductions of human theology, poor at its best estate, consider whether the story of Elisha and his servant has not some significance for you. It is not by demonstration that what seems now only clouds will be disclosed to you horses and chariots of fire. For *you* theology is a snare, and philosophy a delusion. Do you doubt whether the Bible is the inspired Word of God? Do not stop to ascertain. Use it for what it is worth, and in using learn what that worth is. Do you doubt whether Jesus is the Son of God? Do not stop to examine his credentials. Philosophy has no higher argument to offer than that which Philip offered to Nathaniel, "Come and see." Your theology must be the outgrowth of your own experience, not the cast-off clothing of another. Science never solves skepticism. "Oh, taste and see that the Lord is good."

MORDECAI'S TRIUMPH.

## XIV.
## THE QUEEN'S CROWN.

IT is a somewhat singular fact, the explanation of which may be left to those who endeavor to fix certain arbitrary bounds beyond which woman can not pass, that the heroines of Hebrew history are represented as having, almost audaciously, broken over the restraints which the conventionalism of their own age prescribed, in order to fulfill duties to which they were called either by their own extraordinary endowments, or by the peculiar circumstances in which they were placed. Whatever may be thought of "woman's sphere," it is certain that its boundaries have been steadily enlarged; that an increased liberty, not only of secular employments and civil rights, but also of social intercourse, has been accorded to her with increasing civilization; and that, so far from losing, either in the delicacy and refinement of her own character, or in the chivalric homage paid to her by man, she has gained in both respects in the same ratio in which she has been freed from the trammels of an unnatural conventionalism, and elevated to a position of real equality with the dominant sex. Nowhere is she so carefully guarded as in the Orient. Nowhere is she kept in so degrading, so intolerable a bondage. Nowhere is she so free as in America. Nowhere is she held in higher honor; nowhere has she attained a character more worthy the homage paid to her.

The charm of the story of Esther lies in the fact that it portrays the heroism of a woman who thus broke over the rules which society prescribed in order that she might save her nation from destruction, performing with true womanly courage an act which, doubtless, the conventionalism of her age pronounced most unwomanly.

Hadassah, better known by her Persian name of Esther, was born of Jewish parents, but in the land of Persia, at a time of Judah's greatest declension and suffering, and of Persia's greatest power and glory. Her parents died in her infancy. She was adopted by her cousin Mordecai, and brought up by him. Of her early history we know nothing more than this; and of her personal appearance only that she was remarkable, even in that land of beautiful women, for her marvelous beauty.

The Persian throne was occupied by Xerxes, surnamed the Great rather from the grandeur of his domain than from any greatness of character. He was, in fact, an unreasonable, self-willed, capricious, passionate, voluptuous, sensual despot. At the commencement of his reign he displayed, indeed, considerable military ambition. He determined to subjugate Greece. He organized for this purpose an immense army, and marched it across the Hellespont. He anticipated an easy victory; he experienced a humiliating defeat. The winds and waves destroyed his bridge of boats. A storm shattered his fleet. A mere handful of Grecian warriors held his whole army at bay at the Pass of Thermopylæ until treachery gave him the victory which the valor of his troops had been unable to obtain. His whole campaign was marked by deeds of commingled folly, cruelty, and impiety. It was not redeemed by a single generous sentiment or valorous action. He beheaded the engineers who built his bridge across the Hellespont because a storm destroyed it. He punished the presumptuous sea by ordering it to be scourged. His friend Pythias put at the king's disposal his entire fortune. His five sons were in the despot's army. The father requested that the eldest might be suffered to remain at home. The angry monarch responded to the request by slaying the son, and cutting the dead body in two, that the army might march between the dissevered portions. The bravery of Leonidas has rendered his name immortal among all civilized nations and to all time. Xerxes indicated his appreciation of the bravery of his chivalric foe by cutting the head from the dead body and crucifying the headless trunk. At the first serious disaster, like a coward as he was, he fled back to Persia, taking an ample body-guard for his own protection, and leaving Mardonius to extricate the remainder of his army from the toils into which his own folly had led it. Disgraced, but not humbled, he returned to his palace to forget the shame of his inglorious campaign in a more shameful life of self-indulgence. He abandoned the administration of his government to his ministers. He gave himself up to a life of debauchery and vice. By a public edict he offered a prize to the discovery of any new form of pleasure. His drunken orgies lasted continuously for days and even weeks. Least of generals, he became greatest of debauchees. His brother's wife and his son's wife were successively the victims of his amours. His brother and his nephews were successively the victims of his hate. And, finally, he, who had employed mercilessly the assassin's knife, perished himself by the hand of an assassin, after twenty years of a shameful reign.

Such was the king who occupied the throne of Persia at the time our story opens. In secular history he is known as Xerxes. In Scripture he is designated by the Hebrew form of the same word—Ahasuerus.

In the harem of this lecherous tyrant was a woman by the name of Vashti. She had the misfortune to be exceedingly beautiful, and so to be, for the time, a favorite with the king. The love of such a monarch is as dangerous as his hate. Vashti found it so. In one of those drunken carousals which, under the reign of Xerxes, nightly disgraced the palace at Shushan, he ordered Vashti to be brought into the drinking-hall. He was proud of his favorite's beauty, and desired to show his boon companions that his boasting was not idle. We need not give credence to the horrible tradition that he demanded to exhibit her nude form to his drunken court. To ask her to come unveiled, that she might make exhibition of her face in such a scene and to such a crowd, were insult shameful enough to any woman at any time. It was an insult immeasurable in Persia, where the virtuous wife rarely, if ever, unveiled her face in the presence of any but her husband's most intimate and confidential friends. Vashti indignantly refused to submit to this shameful exhibition. The king, inflamed with wine, took counsel of his boon companions, pronounced upon the spot sentence of divorce, and issued a decree making public Vashti's deposition—her apparent humiliation; her real glory.

When the night's orgies were passed, and the king came to himself, he revolted at his own act. It was not the injustice done to a true woman; it was the loss suffered by himself in that his favorite wife was gone. He had not self-respect enough to retract a shameful decree, only just enough to keep him from such honorable inconsistency. His friends, so Josephus tells us, cast about how they might erase the image of Vashti from the monarch's mind. Their method curiously illustrates the temper both of the man and of the times. The officers of his kingdom were directed to collect the fairest maidens of their respective provinces. From them the king was to select a successor to Vashti.

That Mordecai should have sent his niece to compete for the doubtful honors of such a post does not consort with our conceptions of a guardian's duty. A modern Esther would certainly have revolted against a candidateship so degrading. But allowance must be made for the fact that times have changed, and humanity has made progress since. Doubtless the uncle thought it would be an excellent thing for Esther if she could become the favorite of a monarch so august as Xerxes. Perhaps she shared the opinion with him. In the sixteenth century after Christ, Henry the Eighth experienced no difficulty in finding women quite ready to accept the doubtful and dangerous honor of his royal hand. Esther seems to have interposed no objection. Her beauty was quite sufficient to supplant in the royal memory that of Vashti, and she became the favorite of his harem in her predecessor's place. That she was a Jewess no one suspected. Mordecai had shrewdly bid her keep her birth a secret. He accompanied his niece to court; obtained, it would seem, some petty office there, though this is not very clear; sat continually at the outer gate of the king's palace; and continued to maintain much of his old relation of authority over Esther, despite her change of station.

The later years of Xerxes's reign were rife with plots for his assassination. Such a plot, occurring at this time, came to the knowledge of Mordecai. He disclosed it to the young wife, and she, in her turn, to her husband. The would-be assassins were put to death. A record of the whole transaction, with the name of the informer, was preserved in the court archives. But the careless king inquired not narrowly into it. He attributed his escape to Esther. Mordecai was forgotten, and gained nothing by his discovery of the plot.

While these events were occurring, a skillful but unscrupulous courtier was steadily climbing to the first place in the kingdom. This was Haman, an Amalekite by descent, who shared with his nation its long-nurtured hate of the Israelitish people. Cunning, vain, cowardly, and vengeful, he possessed that peculiar power which self-control gives to wickedness as well as to virtue. Passionately fond of display, he yet contrived to gratify his vanity without avowing it. Participating, without a scruple, in the shameful orgies of the king, he yet preserved his own sobriety, and never lost sight of his own ulterior purposes. Hating whomsoever crossed his path with a persistence which the brutally passionate king could never comprehend, he could yet hide his hate till his measures for a more than fiendish revenge were fully consummated. Crafty in purpose, and sinuous in action, he was an insincere friend, and an inveterate, though a secret and complaisant foe. Such a man readily acquires control of one whose wickedness is that of unregulated impulses rather than of deliberate design. Haman's influence over Xerxes was unbounded. Foreigner though he was, he supplanted all the native princes, and obtained the very highest rank in the kingdom. The Persians are a sycophantic race. To this rising star all the satellites of an obsequious court rendered their homage.

In this universal adulation paid to Haman, Mordecai alone remained decorously, but scornfully erect and haughty. A Pharisee, in an age when Phariseeism had not yet degenerated from a sturdy principle to a stereotyped form, he possessed that defiant self-respect, and that robust, though somewhat narrow conscience which rendered the Puritan, two thousand years later, so rigidly virtuous. Between two such characters there always arises a bitter hatred—a principle in the one, a passion in the other. The Jew despised the cunning but treacherous complaisance of the Amalekite. The Amalekite hated the rigorous virtue and inflexible pride of the Jew. It was the Cavalier against the Puritan, the Jesuit against the Huguenot. Haman waited his time, and nursed his wrath, which grew with the nursing to hideous proportions. Patience in passion is the very climax of wickedness. He determined to avenge the insults he had received by obliterating with one cruel stroke the entire Jewish population of the empire.

The Jews were then, as now, a thrifty people. Haman calculated that the extermination of this captive race, and the confiscation of their estates, would put into the royal treasury over ten millions of dollars. He seized a favorable opportunity for proposing this scheme to Xerxes. He was so confident of the result that he proposed to pay the sum out of his own coffers. The king's funds were exhausted by excessive and increasing luxury and dissipation. He cared little about the lives of a few thousand of his subjects. If his conscience considered the matter at all, it was satisfied by the fact that this foreign people worshiped their own God, maintained their own religious rites, and preserved, even in their captivity, their own peculiar code of laws. With the capriciousness of a despot who does not care to trouble himself about affairs of state, he took off his royal ring, and gave it to Haman: "Do with them," said he, "as it seemeth good unto thee." The decree was issued accordingly. It provided for the absolute extermination of all the Jews within Xerxes's domain. It was posted in the palace. It was sent out by couriers to every province. Then Haman and the king sat down to ratify it in a drinking bout.

To remonstrate was idle. Pythias had proved that. The

Jews gave themselves up to irremediable grief. Mordecai wore sackcloth even at the king's gate. The careless despot never noticed his servant's strange attire; never, at least, asked its meaning. The Persian court, guarding its pleasures against every intrusion, forbade the entrance within the palace of all such symbols of sorrow. Meanwhile Esther, in her seclusion, was quite ignorant of the decree. She first learned its terms from Mordecai. He sent her a copy of the edict. At the same time, he called upon her to intercede with her husband for her people. Of course he had no admission to the harem, she no exit from it. A faithful servant carried their messages to and fro.

Esther hesitated. To enter uninvited the royal presence was to break over all the rules of court etiquette, disregard all the proprieties of Persian life, overstep the very bounds of womanly reserve. Nor was it safe to venture much on the favor of this capricious king. A single crossing of his will drove Vashti from her throne. And yet the judgment of the monarch, when sober, must have condemned the decree issued by the monarch when drunk. Already Esther's power seemed to be weakened. It was thirty days since she had seen the king. Persian law hedged royalty about with peculiar dignity. To enter its presence unbidden was a capital offense. To Esther it seemed an act audacious—like entering the very court of death itself.

To her remonstrances Mordecai returned a simple but significant reply. It curiously interprets the character of the man. It is such an answer as a Cromwell might have given to his daughter. "Think not with thyself that thou shalt escape in the king's house more than all the Jews. For if thou altogether holdest thy peace at this time, then shall there enlargement and deliverance arise to the Jews from another place; but thou and thy father's house shall be destroyed; and who knoweth whether thou art come to the kingdom for such a time as this?"

He had read his adopted daughter's character correctly. She prepared to fulfill the service required of her. She bade Mordecai gather the Jews of Shushan together, and observe three days of prayer and fasting. She, with her Jewish maidens, observed them also within the palace walls. Then she laid aside all emblems of her grief. She schooled herself utterly to conceal its every indication. She understood the king's weaknesses. She prepared a banquet of wine for him. She attired herself with unusual care in her royal apparel, making the most of her extraordinary beauty. Then she crossed the threshold of the harem, traversed the court that separated it from the main hall of the palace, pushed her way through the throng of surprised courtiers and attendants, and stood in the doorway of the throne-room, waiting with beating heart the signal that should give hope of life to her nation, or should decree death to both it and her.

The moment is auspicious, the king in gracious mood. He holds out his sceptre, signal of favor. She draws near to touch it, then prefers her request. It is simply that the king will honor with his presence her banquet of wine. Will he also be pleased to bring his favorite minister,

Haman, with him. The king will be pleased to do so. He descends from his throne. The minister and his master sit together at the table Esther has prepared for them. But she is still reticent. Pressed by the king to declare her request, she simply repeats her invitation. Will the king and Haman do her the honor to partake upon the morrow of another banquet? She will then make known her petition. The king promises. The banquet draws to its close. The monarch and his minister depart. The first and hardest step is taken.

Haman is completely duped. He goes home elated. He has enjoyed the highest honor which the king can bestow upon him. He has sat at the same table with his favorite wife. Whether he has really secured the favor of that wife, or whether she is seeking to secure his, he cares not. In either case his power is equally assured. The dream of his ambition is already realized. The very envy of his fellows enhances the subtle exhilaration of his dainty vanity. One thing alone detracts from it. Mordecai still stands at the king's gate. His people are condemned to die. He will die with them. The signs of sorrow are written in his face. The uncomely sackcloth constitutes his dress. But he is as erect as ever, and repays the fiery glance of hate that leaps from Haman's eyes with scorn invincible. Haman's revenge loses its patience. He can no longer wait till the appointed day of death shall come. Mordecai shall die upon the morrow. That very night the gallows for his execution are erected.

That very night the king, strangely sleepless, bids the

chamberlains read for his entertainment from the records of the court. They hap to read the story of his preservation by Mordecai from the assassin's knife. What has been done to Mordecai? Nothing. What shall be done? Xerxes is still pondering this question when Haman enters, in the morning, to ask for Mordecai's execution. The king is first to speak. "What shall be done," he says, "to the man whom the king delighteth to honor?" Revenge is sweet, but the intoxication of a gratified vanity is sweeter to this Amalekite. Besides, the gallows can wait. And that he is the one whom the king delighteth to honor the curiously self-conceited soul of Haman never doubts. So he sketches for the king the display he covets.

"For the man whom the king delighteth to honor," he replies, "let the royal apparel be brought which the king useth to wear, and the horse that the king rideth upon, and the crown royal which is set upon his head; and let this apparel and horse be delivered to the hand of one of the king's most noble princes, that they may array the man withal whom the king delighteth to honor, and bring him on horseback through the street of the city, and proclaim before him, 'Thus shall it be done to the man whom the king delighteth to honor.'"

Well said, wise counselor. Wherefore make haste, and take the apparel and the horse, as thou hast said, and do even so to Mordecai the Jew, that sitteth at the king's gate.

Thunderstruck and speechless, Haman proceeds to execute the king's commission. He proclaims, through the streets of the capital, royal honors to the man whose gallows he had the night before constructed; then, in a tempest of humiliated pride, of hot and hardly restrained rage, and of shadowy fear, he hurries home. His obsequious followers drop away from him. Even his wife taunts him. He has no clear conception of the dangers thickening around him, no self-reliant courage to meet them if he had. He is still counseling with his friends when the chamberlains come to hasten him to Esther's banquet. He has not, then, lost caste at court. He will yet retrieve himself. Encouraging himself with this hope, despite some dark forebodings of unknown calamities yet to come, he hastens back to the palace. Again the king and his favorite courtier sit down at the table of the beautiful Esther. Again the king repeats his question, "What is thy petition, Queen Esther? and it shall be granted thee; and what is thy request? and it shall be performed to the half of the kingdom."

Then Esther, with the impassioned eloquence of the woman, and the courtly bearing of the queen, pleads for her life, and the life of her people, and the life of Mordecai, the king's deliverer. The careless monarch has already forgotten the decree wheedled from him in a drunken orgy. His passion is something terrible to witness. "Who is he, and where is he," he cries, "that durst presume in his heart to do so?" All the pent-up scorn of the woman's lacerated heart bursts forth in her fierce indictment of "the adversary and enemy, this wicked Haman." The king, too angry to speak, rises from the table, and goes out to the cool of the garden to collect his thoughts. The craven-hearted Haman, groveling in the very abjectness of his fear, falls down on Esther's couch, beseeching for his life. Such cowardice has no power to awaken compassion. She shrinks from the pollution of his touch. The king, returning, pretends to believe that Haman is threatening her with violence before his eyes. "Will he force the queen also before me in the house?" he cries. This is sentence of condemnation enough. In all the court, obsequious as it has been, Haman has not a single true and trusty friend. Every heart exults in his downfall. Eager are the hands that bear him away to hang him on the gallows he had prepared for Mordecai.

An absurd provision of the Persian constitution prohibited the repeal of any decree, however odious. Even Xerxes could not retract the edict which Haman had promulgated under the royal seal. A second decree was therefore issued. It authorized the Jews to stand their ground, to defend themselves against their enemies, and so to preserve their lives which had been declared forfeited. A brief but sanguinary conflict ensued. The moral influence of the court was with the Jews. They were victorious. But it was not until over seventy-five thousand of their enemies had been slain. It is a Jewish tradition that the entire Amalekitish people perished in this conflict. The deliverance of the Jews is celebrated in their synagogues to the present day by a national feast, and the book of Esther is held by them in reverence second only to that which is accorded to the Pentateuch itself.

In our reverence for the higher Christian experiences we are apt to forget the homelier virtues. In these later days, when the qualities of amiableness, and gentleness, and charity toward all mankind are so exclusively praised, we are apt to slight the rarer virtue of true courage, which there is little to call forth. The ruggedness of the Puritan is not pleasing. We scarcely consider that he whose life is a campaign must needs wear a coat of mail. Yet nothing is more certain than that courage is a Christian virtue, and that a cowardly Christian is an anomaly in theory, however common it may seem to be in actual life. Christianity has been rightly entitled "a battle, not a dream." There are many heroes of the night, who win great victories, perform great achievements, but never leave the pillow. It is not thus "sleeping the hours away" that we are to gain our crown. Without courage to do, to dare, to suffer, there is neither victory here nor coronation hereafter. Courage is the alchemist who transmutes noble aspirations into a noble life. It is not enough that we revere Christ. We must follow him, if need be, to Gethsemane and to Calvary; through the midnight hour of agonizing prayer, the shame and spitting of the judgment-hall, the protracted anguish of the crucifixion. "Be thou faithful unto death, and I will give thee a crown of life." Courage is the Christian's coronation. There is no crown without it.

"Let us run with patience the race that is set before us." This is the message which Esther brings us. This is generally the last thing we are willing to do. We are quite ready to run, with most exemplary patience, every race but our own; to fight every battle but the particular one to which God has called us. It is not only that we dread the danger, shrink from the rugged path; but we mark our deficiencies, account ourselves ill adapted to the work, answer to the call of God as Moses did, entreat him to find another candidate for work which we consider too difficult for our capacities.

Esther, timid, tender, retiring, dependent on her cousin even after she became a queen, was not the woman you would have chosen to be the deliverer of her people. But God adapts his instruments to their work. He is with Moses's mouth, and teaches him what he shall say. He gives Esther the courage and the rare self-control when the critical and trying hour comes. It is always safe to run the race which God sets before us. We need not trouble ourselves overmuch about our capacities. His promise is, "As thy days, so shall thy strength be." Whatever duty, then, God lays upon you, do it bravely, manfully, unhesitatingly. The issue is in his hands. The responsibility is his. If you can look back upon exigencies in life when, for Christ's sake, you have taken up a difficult duty, faced a real danger, you can bear witness that the lions are always chained. If you have had no such experience, it is time you had it. God often gives us tasks we think too great for us, as a teacher gives his pupil a problem that tries his powers to the uttermost, just that he may prove us, and see what is our mettle. If a duty too arduous, if a path too dangerous lie before you, ask yourself this question, "Who knoweth whether thou art come to the kingdom for such a time as this?"

Esther's history has its prophetic meaning too. Turn your eyes for one moment from this national deliverance to the grander one it typifies. See a race in bondage; foreigners in a strange land, lying under sentence of death— but sentence justly deserved. See a great Deliverer not only hazarding, but freely giving his life a ransom for many. Hear, in Esther's prayer, the faint echo of his who ever liveth and maketh intercession for us. Well might the Jewish nation hold in immortal honor this Esther, whose more than queenly courage saved their race from destruction. Well may we hold thee, O Christ, in immortal honor, whose plea has annulled the inexorable edict, and given us deliverance.

> "Interceding
> With these bleeding
> Wounds upon thy hands and feet,
> For all who have lived and erred
> Thou hast suffered, thou hast died,
> Scourged, and mocked, and crucified,
> And in the grave hast thou been buried."

---

A golden thread, woven into the Old Testament history, renders the various lives whose stories it recounts only different phases of the same experience. That golden thread is faith. Not faith in the atoning blood of a Savior; the patriarchs knew nothing—certainly nothing clear or definite—of a Savior. Not faith in the dogmas of the Church; the creed did not assume its present form until several centuries after Christ, some of its tenets not till the Reformation. But faith in God; faith that he is, and is the rewarder of them that diligently seek him; faith, the substance of things hoped for, the evidence of things not seen; this, the common blood of all the children of God, whatever their creed, their Church, their age, or their nation, makes of them all one household.

The shortest, but most significant biography in the Bible is the sentence, "Enoch walked with God." This sentence reveals the secret power which made the lives of Abraham, of Moses, of David, of the prophets illustrious. Mr. Lecky is right in saying, "Among Christians, the ideals have commonly been either supernatural beings, or men who were in constant connection with supernatural beings." The very teaching of the Scriptures is this, that every man should live in constant and intimate connexion with his heavenly Father; that he is not made to live by bread alone, but by every word, or, as the Germans express it, by "the all" which proceedeth from the mouth of God; that the Spirit of God acts immediately and directly upon the human soul, strengthening its courage, quickening its moral sense, enlightening its judgment, inspiring all its faculties with peculiar power, and enabling it constantly to do, to bear, to suffer what elsewise would be far beyond its capacities. They measure the human soul, not by its inherent powers, but by its readiness to receive and profit by this divine companionship; not by its native wisdom, courage, or goodness, but by its faith. It is this which gives to Hebrew history its peculiar charm, and makes it dear to thousands of readers who are ignorant of Tacitus, of Herodotus, of Plutarch. The whole Bible culminates in one word, Immanuel—God with us. The Bible heroes are not in other respects grander than some of the heroes of heathen antiquity. Their peculiar characteristic is their susceptibility to divine influence. Their goodness is all the product of godliness. Through weakness they are made strong by the indwelling Spirit of God. "There is no Marathon, no Regillus, no Tours, no Morgarten. All is from above, nothing from themselves." Eliezer is not celebrated for his own sagacity. God guides him. Joseph does not provide Egypt with plenty by his own forecasting. The prophecy and the plan are God's. Moses is not eloquent. God is with his mouth. Samson is vanquished because his strength is godless; is victorious in the hour when weakness has driven him to God. Esther was courageous because God is invincible.

Faith has not lost its power. The soul still enjoys this privilege of receiving inspiration from above. It is not the special prerogative of a few saints. It is the common right of all. It is not an occasional, exceptional gift. It is constant, continuous, the law of our being. It is not a miracle, interfering with the operations of the human soul. It is the condition of our soul's true life. "In him we live, and move, and have our being." God is our native air. The godless soul gasps out a feeble life in a vacuum. "I will not leave you orphans," saith Christ; "I will come to you." Yet, despite this promise, how many orphaned Christians there are. They are not exactly fatherless. They have a memory of a father in the dim past. They have a hope of a Father in the far future. But now they live without him. They are like travelers in a long and gloomy tunnel. They look back to the days of the patriarchs and prophets. There is light there. They look forward to the revelations of the future life. There is light there. But here and now it is dark.

Oh, fellow-Christian, there is for us something better than this. There is a present, helpful God. To us is repeated the promise he made to Moses, "My presence shall go with thee, and I will give thee rest." He is our shield and buckler as well as David's. He is now, as then, a *present* help in time of trouble. It is as true as when Isaiah wrote, "They that wait upon the Lord shall renew their strength." This is the meaning of these various lives, this the moral they have for us. The Bible celebrates not the strength of a Hercules, the wisdom of a Solon, the valor of a Hector, the self-sacrificing patriotism of a Regulus, the matronly virtue of a Cornelia, but that faith in God, the common heritage of all his children, which endows Moses with wisdom greater than that of the Grecian law-giver, Joshua with a valor more inspiring than that of the hero of Homer's verses, and which alike irradiates the life of Joseph, the peasant king, and Eliezer, the faithful servant; Esther, deliverer of her people, and Ruth, in her humble sphere, a faithful friend. These all testify to the power of that faith which endures, as seeing him who is invisible. In them all the Spirit of God, abiding, points with prophetic promise to him in whom dwelleth all the fullness of the Godhead bodily, and who is, far above all others, our pattern and example, chiefly in this, that he did nothing of himself, but the Father that dwelleth within him, he did the works.

"Wherefore, seeing we also are compassed about with so great a cloud of witnesses, let us lay aside every weight, and the sin which doth so easily beset us, and let us run with patience the race that is set before us, looking unto Jesus, the author and finisher of faith; who, for the joy that was set before him, endured the cross, despising the shame, and is set down at the right hand of the throne of God."

www.ingramcontent.com/pod-product-compliance
Lightning Source LLC
Chambersburg PA
CBHW020859230426
43666CB00008B/1244